BADLY
T**I**MED
BONERS

Published in 2015 by Prion
An imprint of the Carlton Publishing Group
20 Mortimer Street
London W1T 3JW

A CIP catalogue record for this book is available from the British Library.

Editorial: Roland Hall
Design: James Pople
Production: Marion Storz

Printed in China

ISBN 978 1 85375 945 1

10 9 8 7 6 5 4 3 2

BADLY TIMED BONERS

by Jolyon White

PRION

Introduction

All men know what it's like to get that feeling; you can't control when or where it happens. You think of all sorts of off-putting things in the hope that it goes before you cause an awkward scene, but as you'll see that isn't always the case. . .

Jolyon White

For Ellen

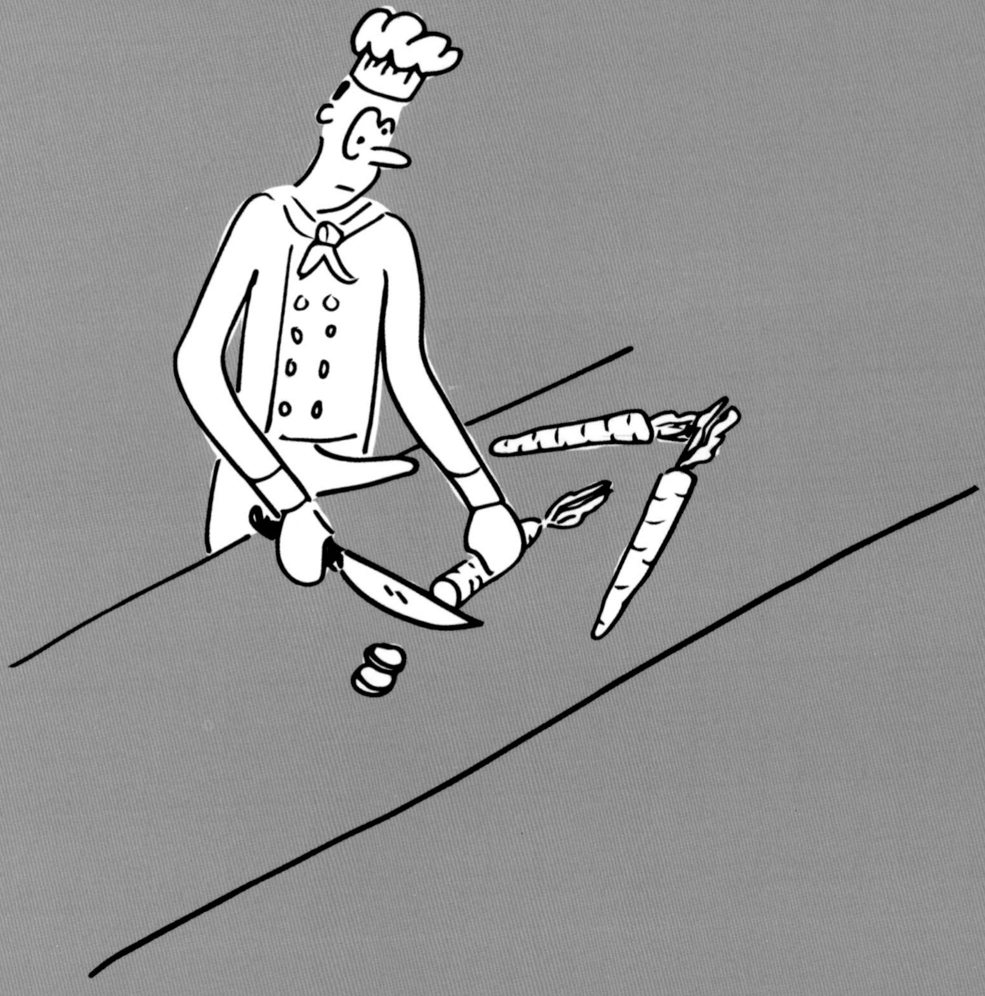

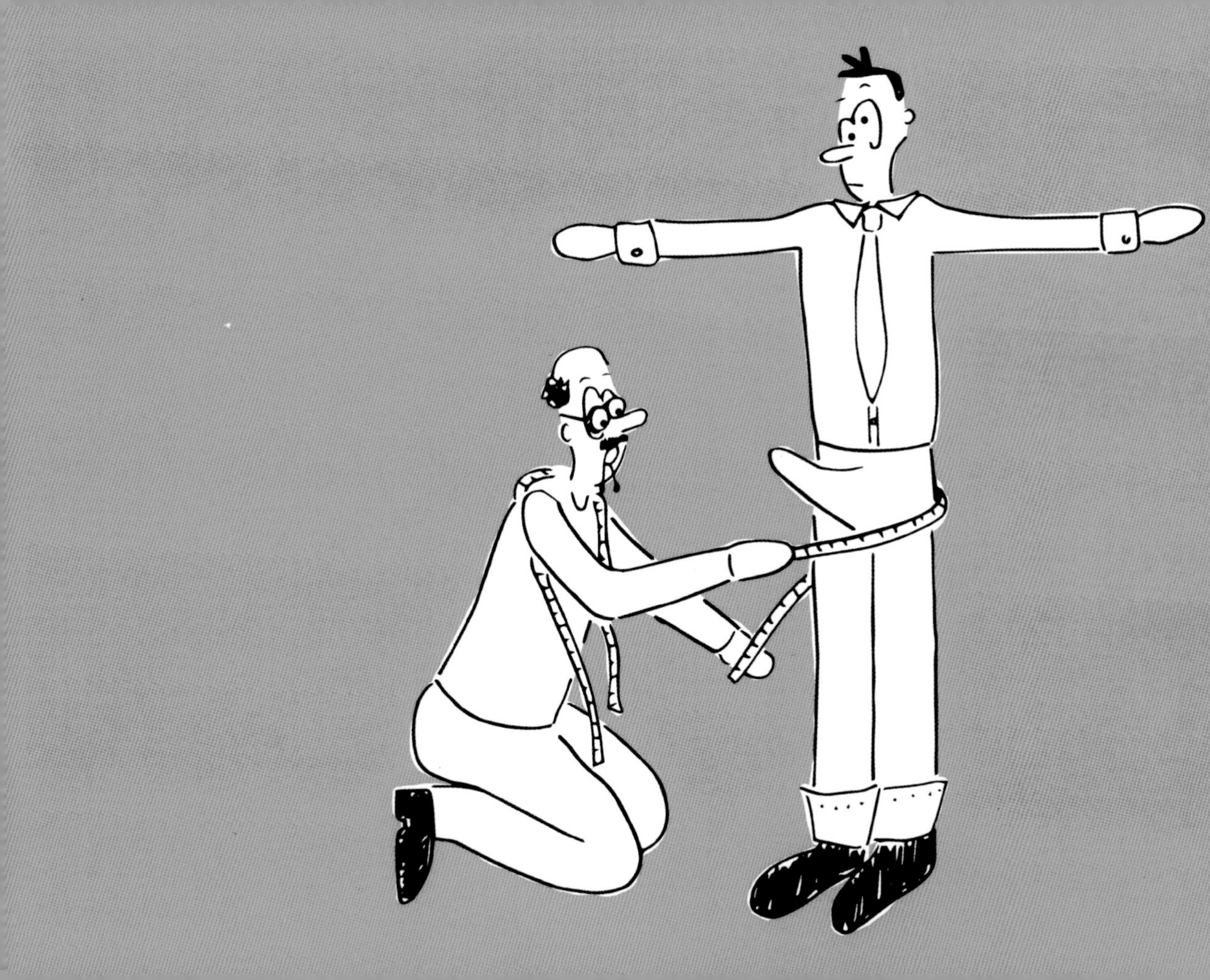

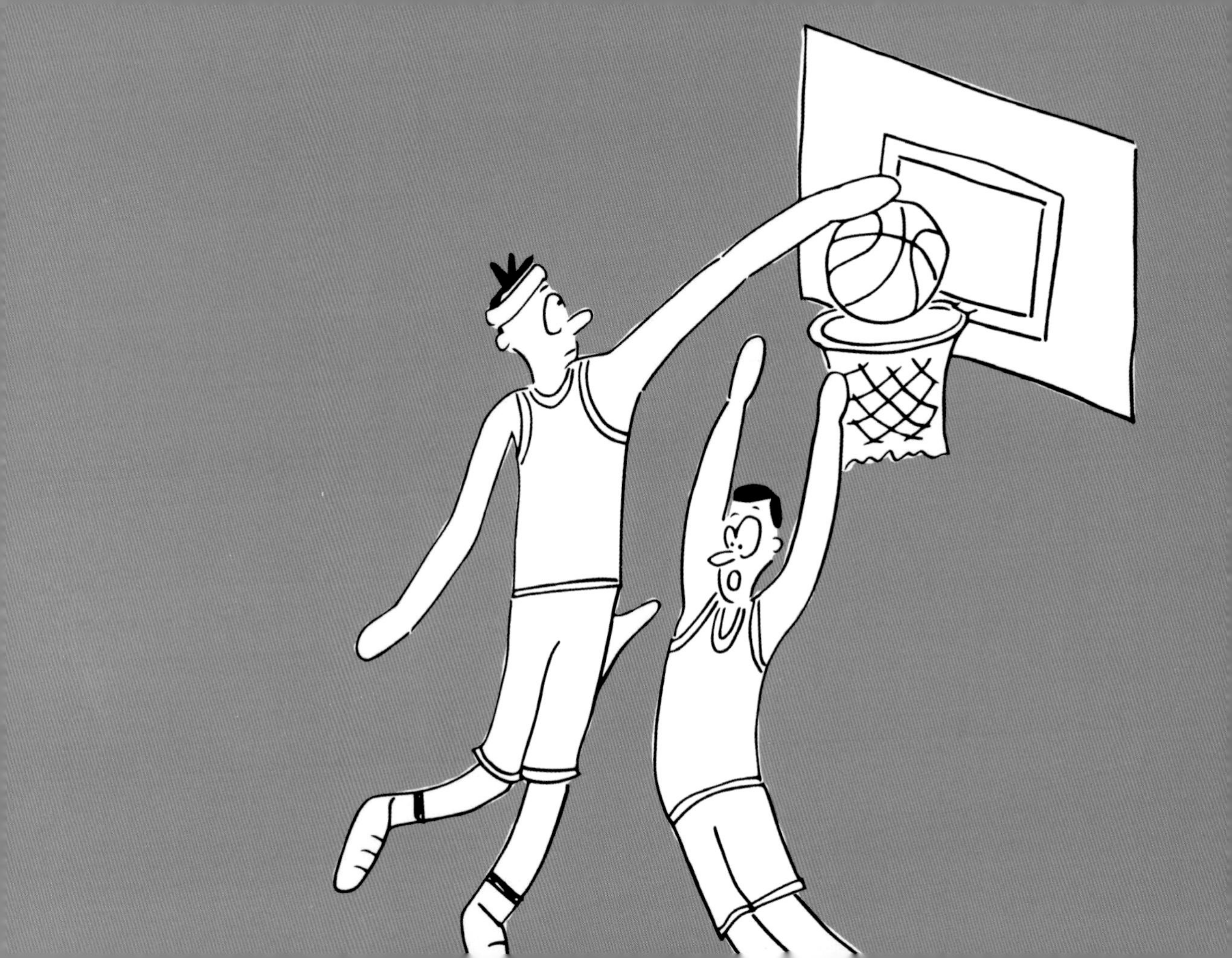

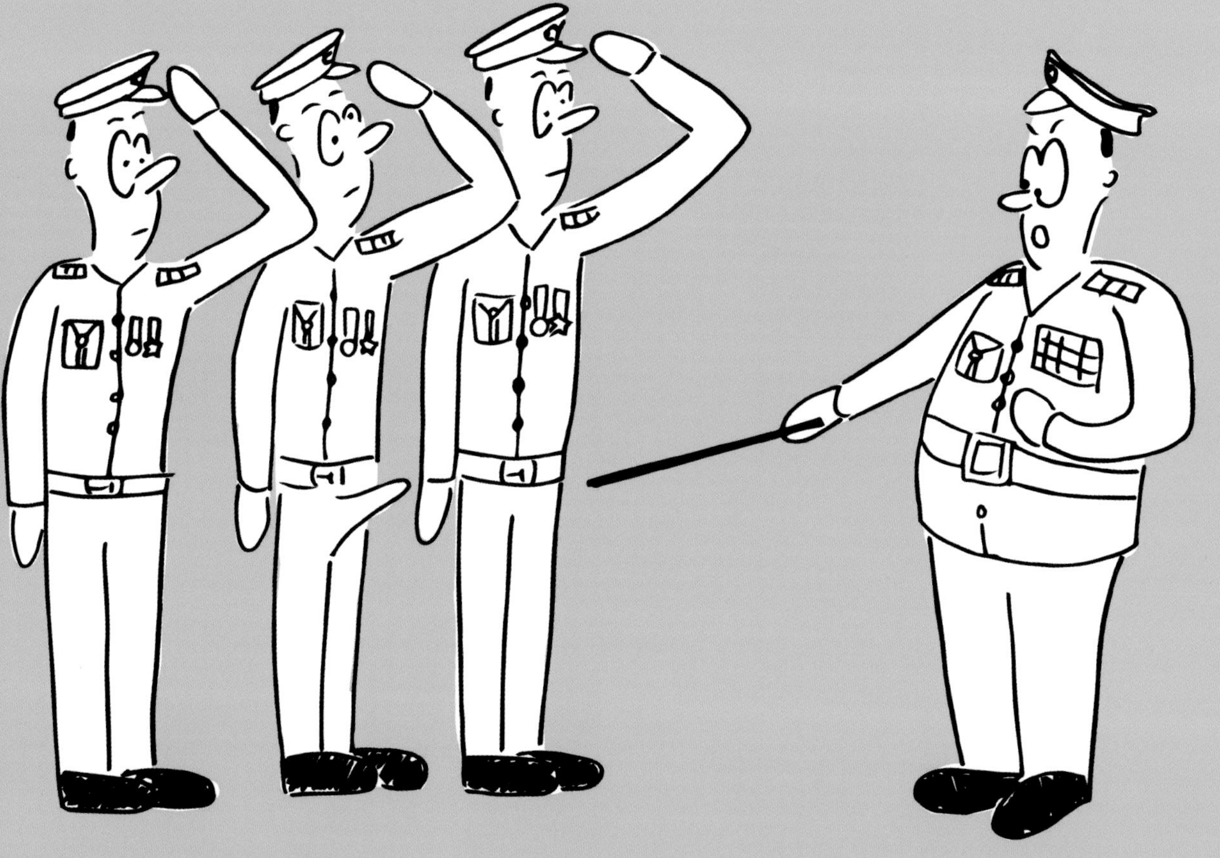

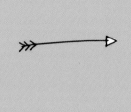

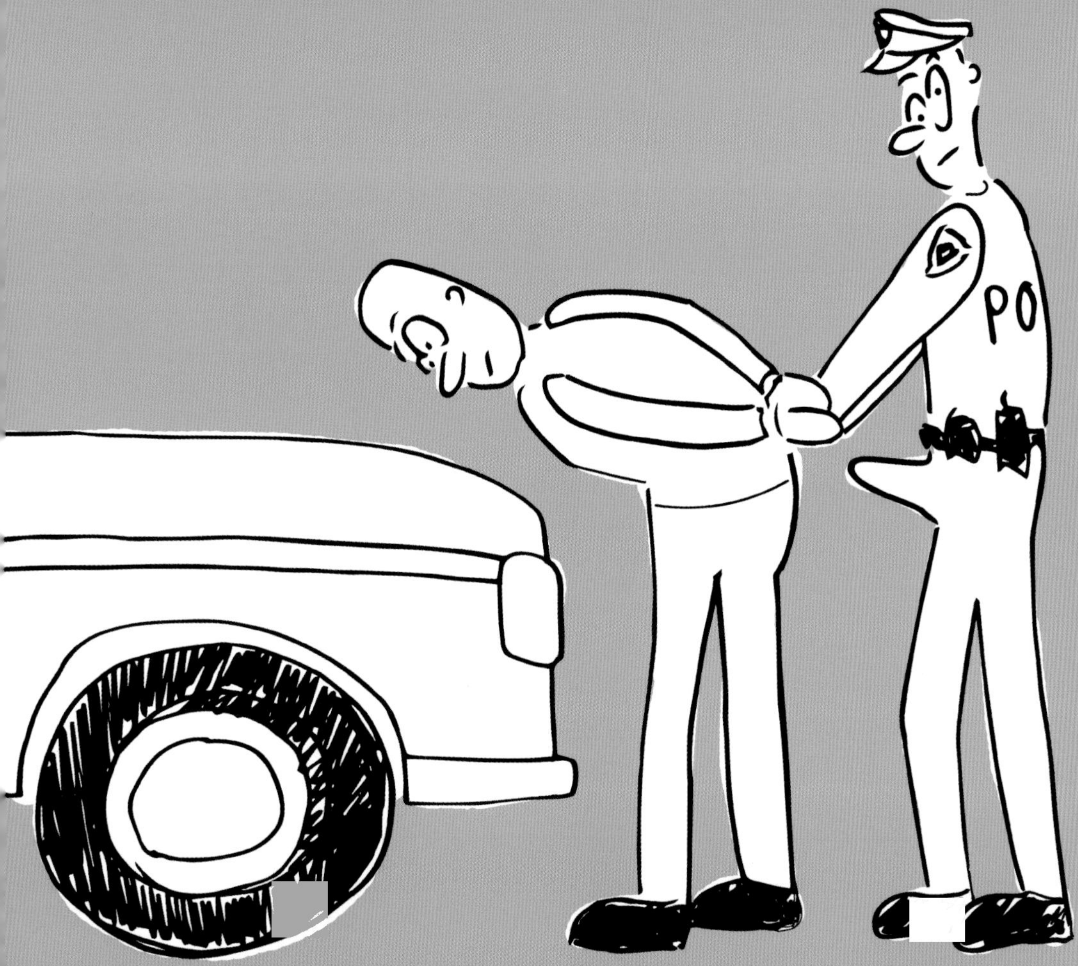
PO

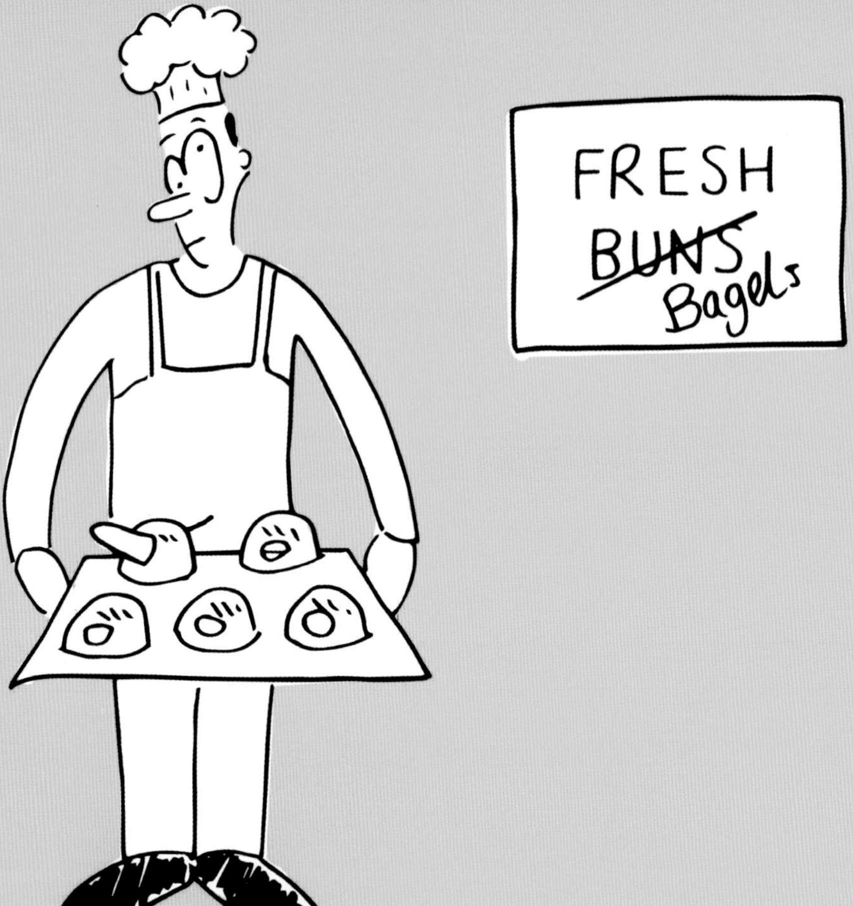
FRESH
~~BUNS~~
Bagels

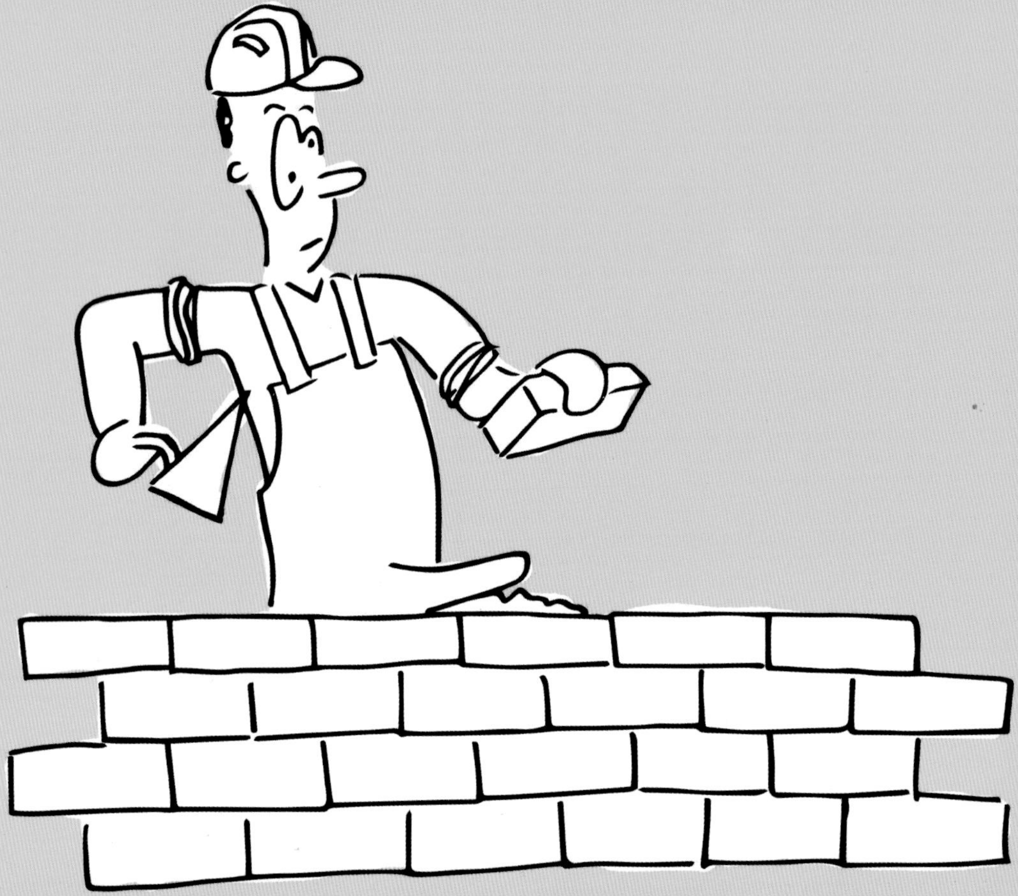

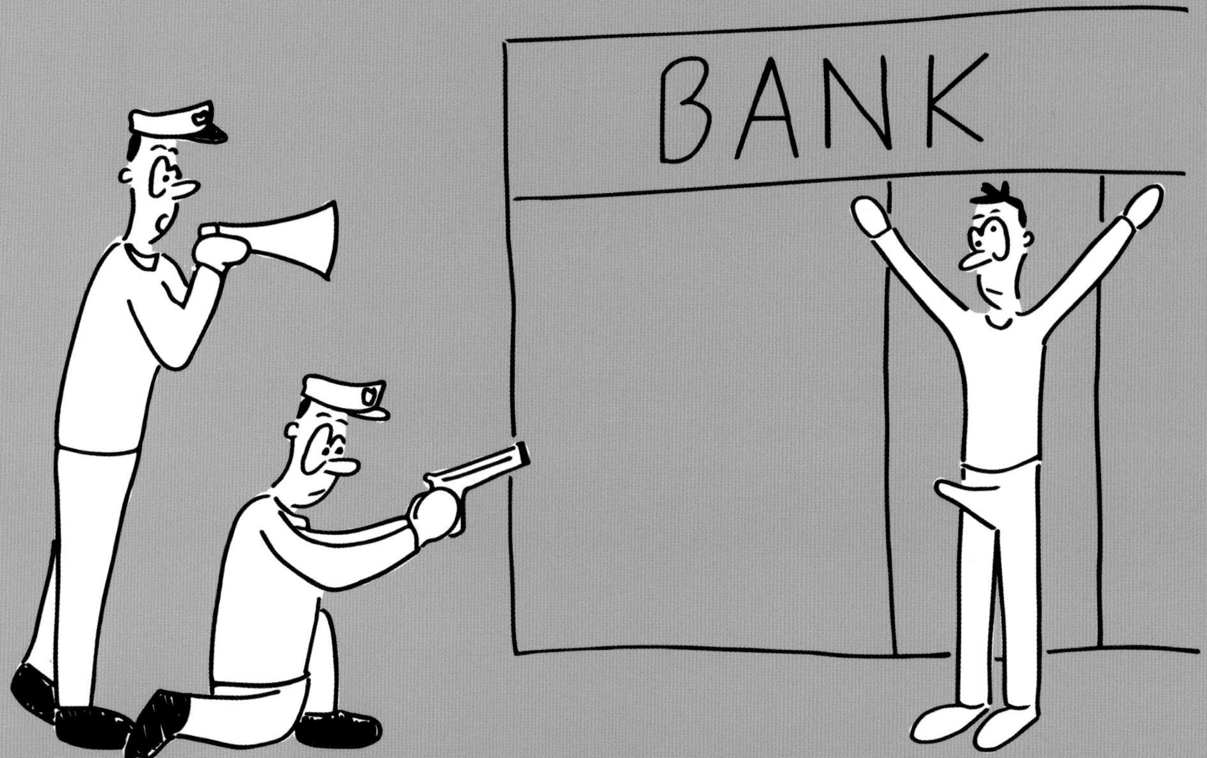
BANK

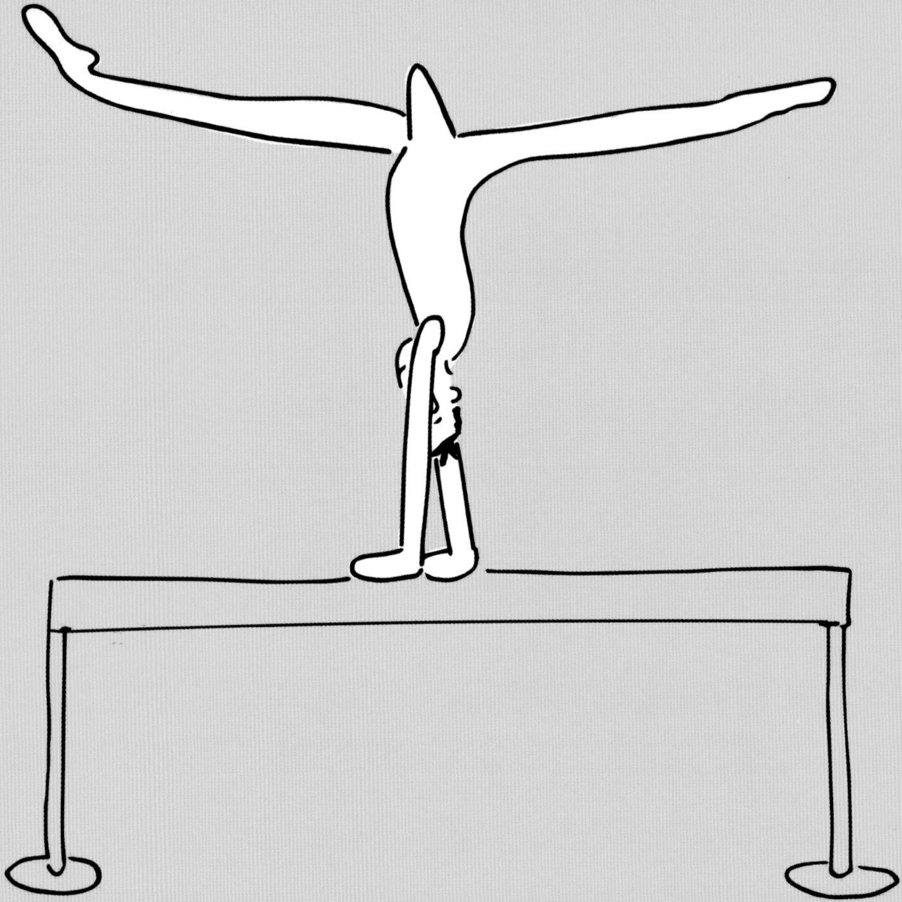

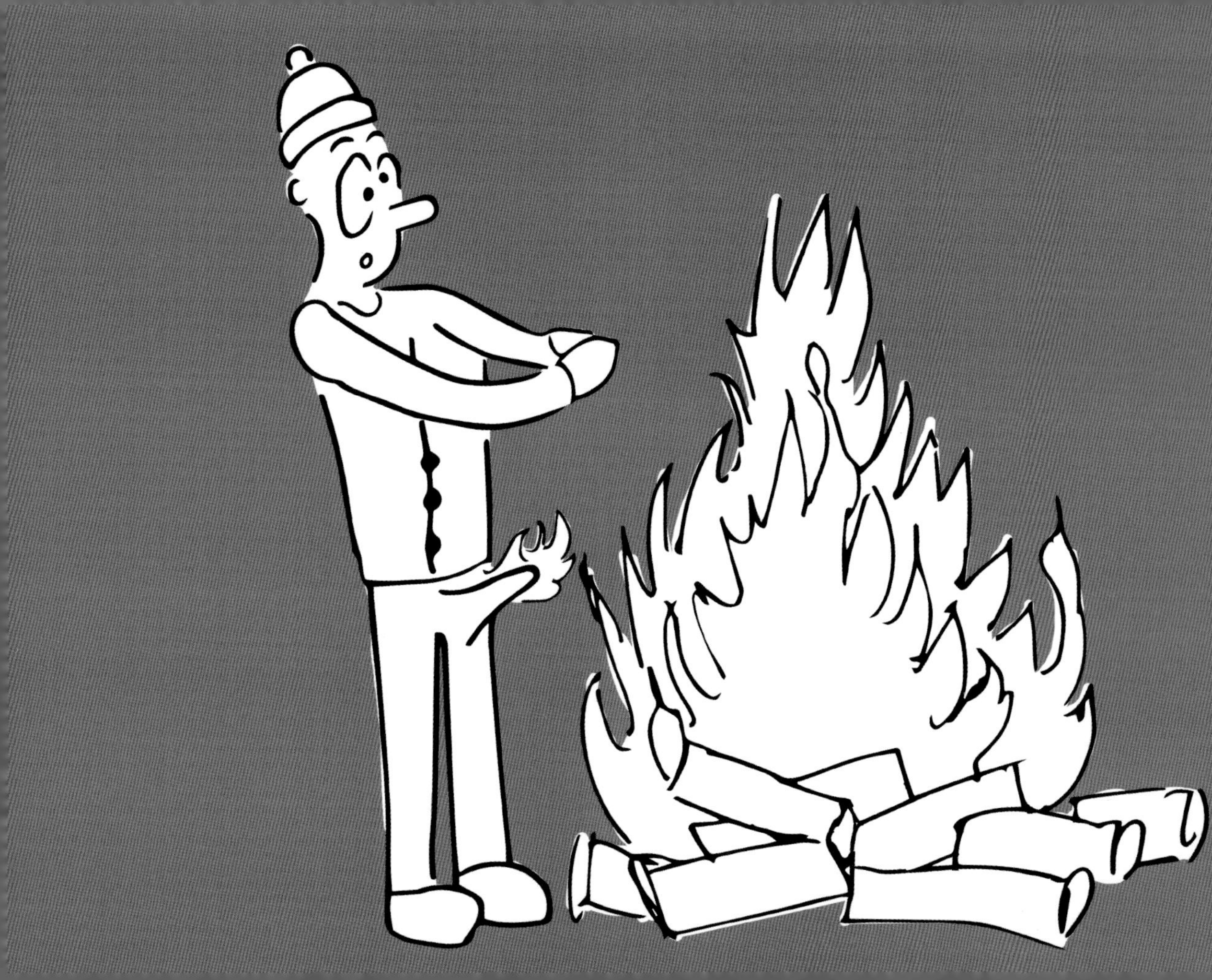

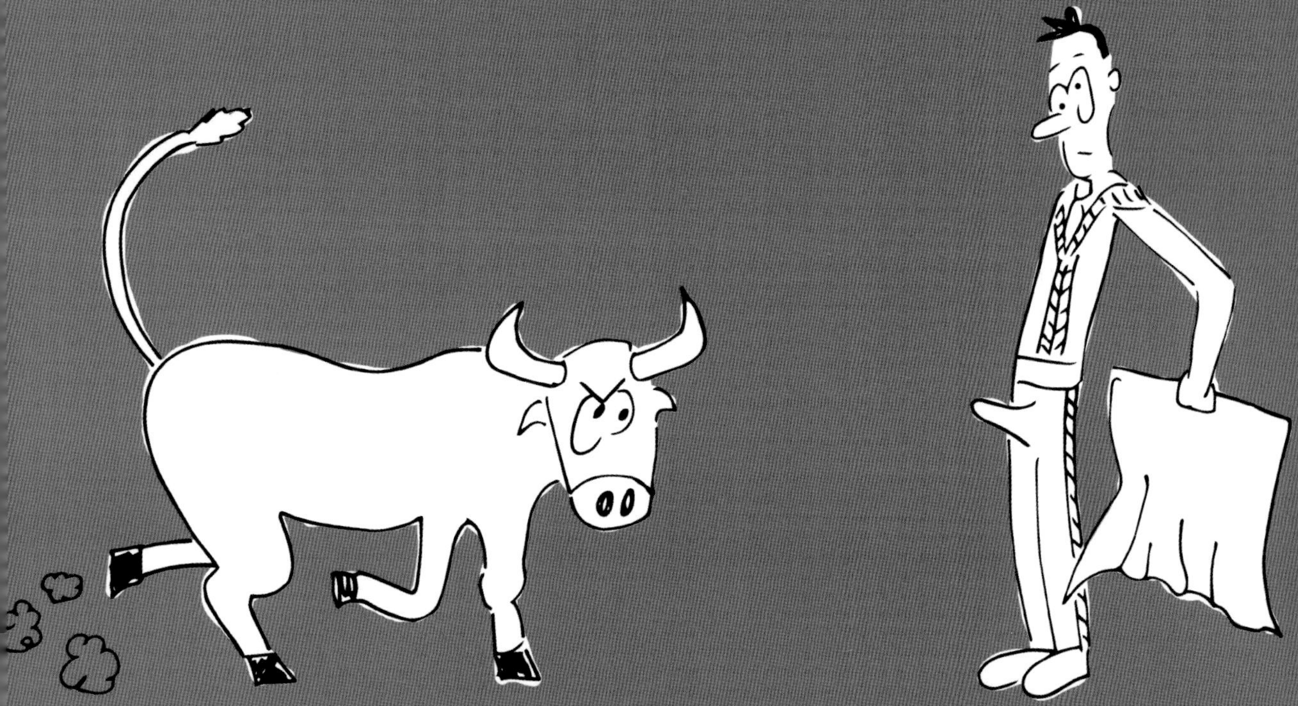

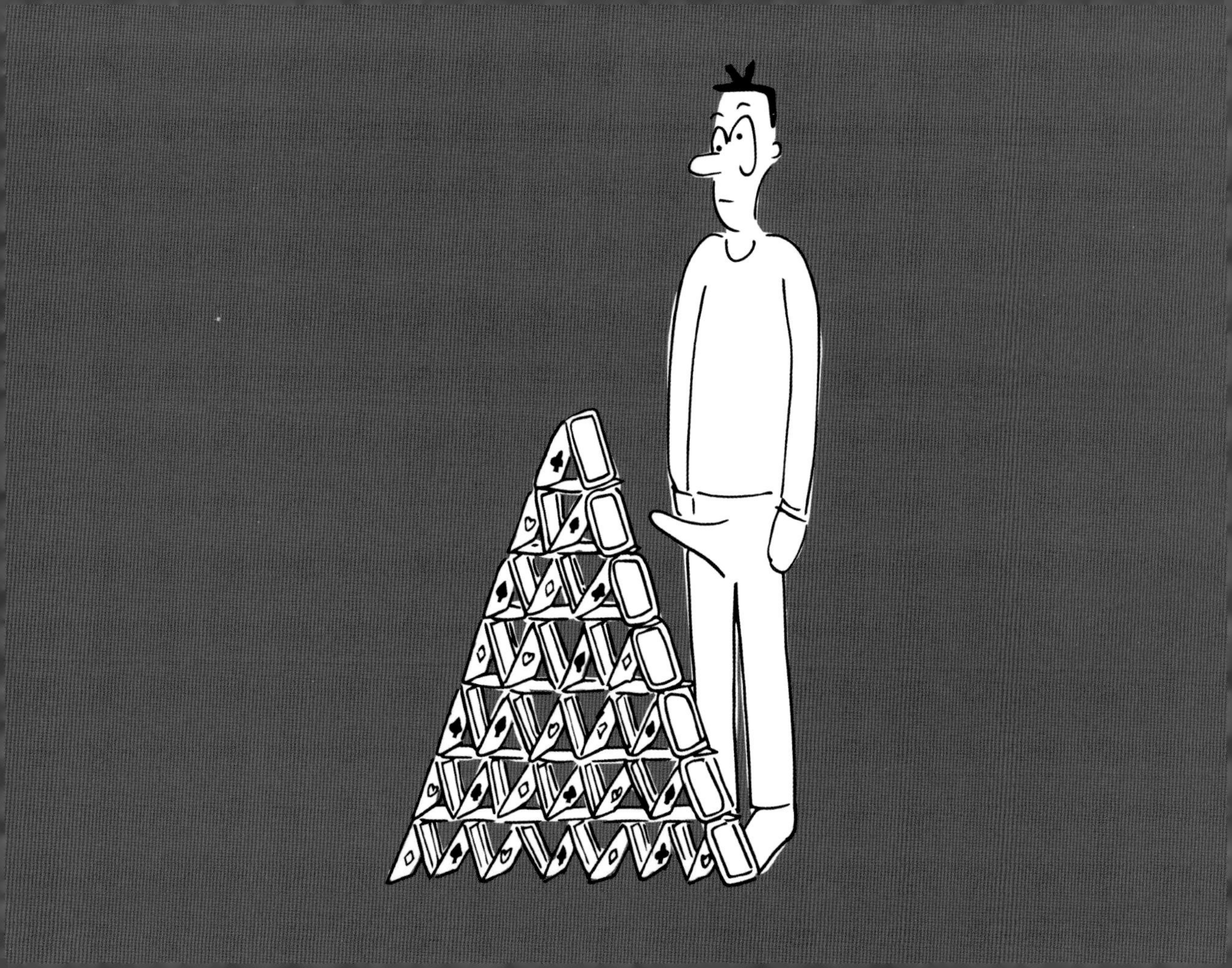

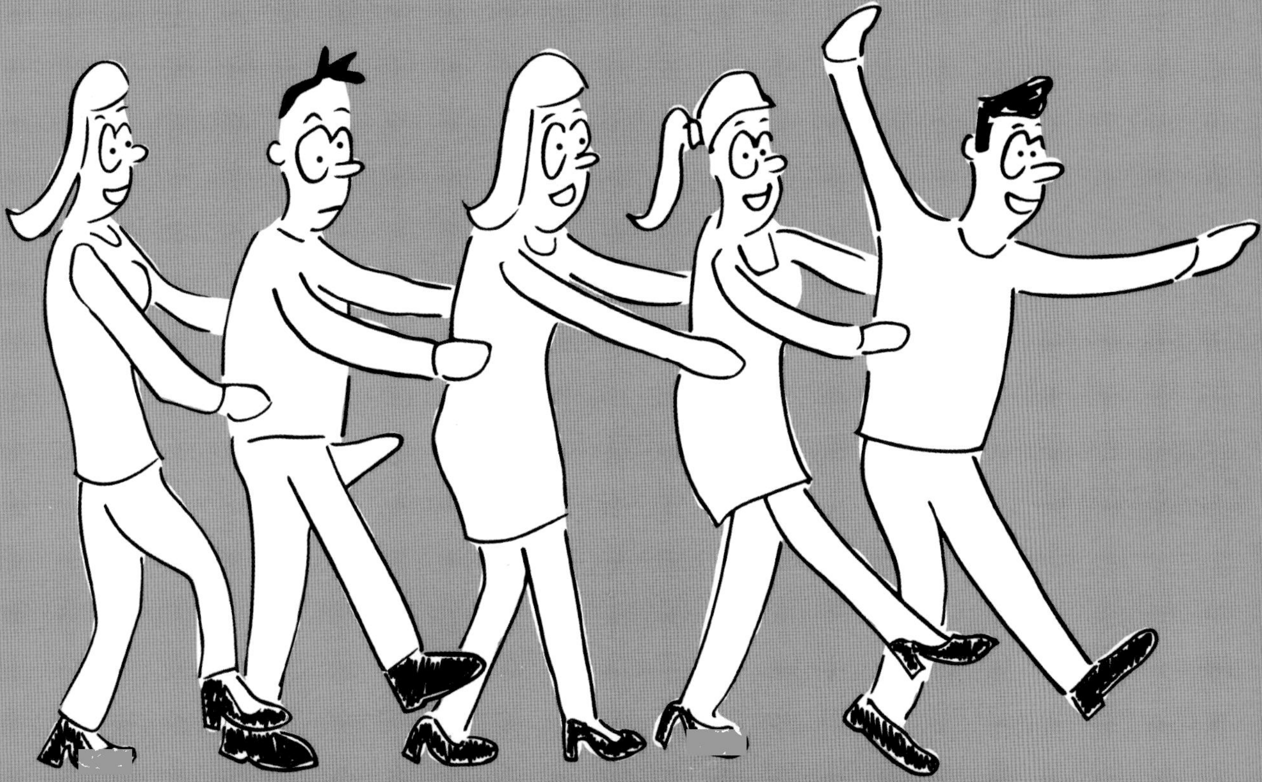

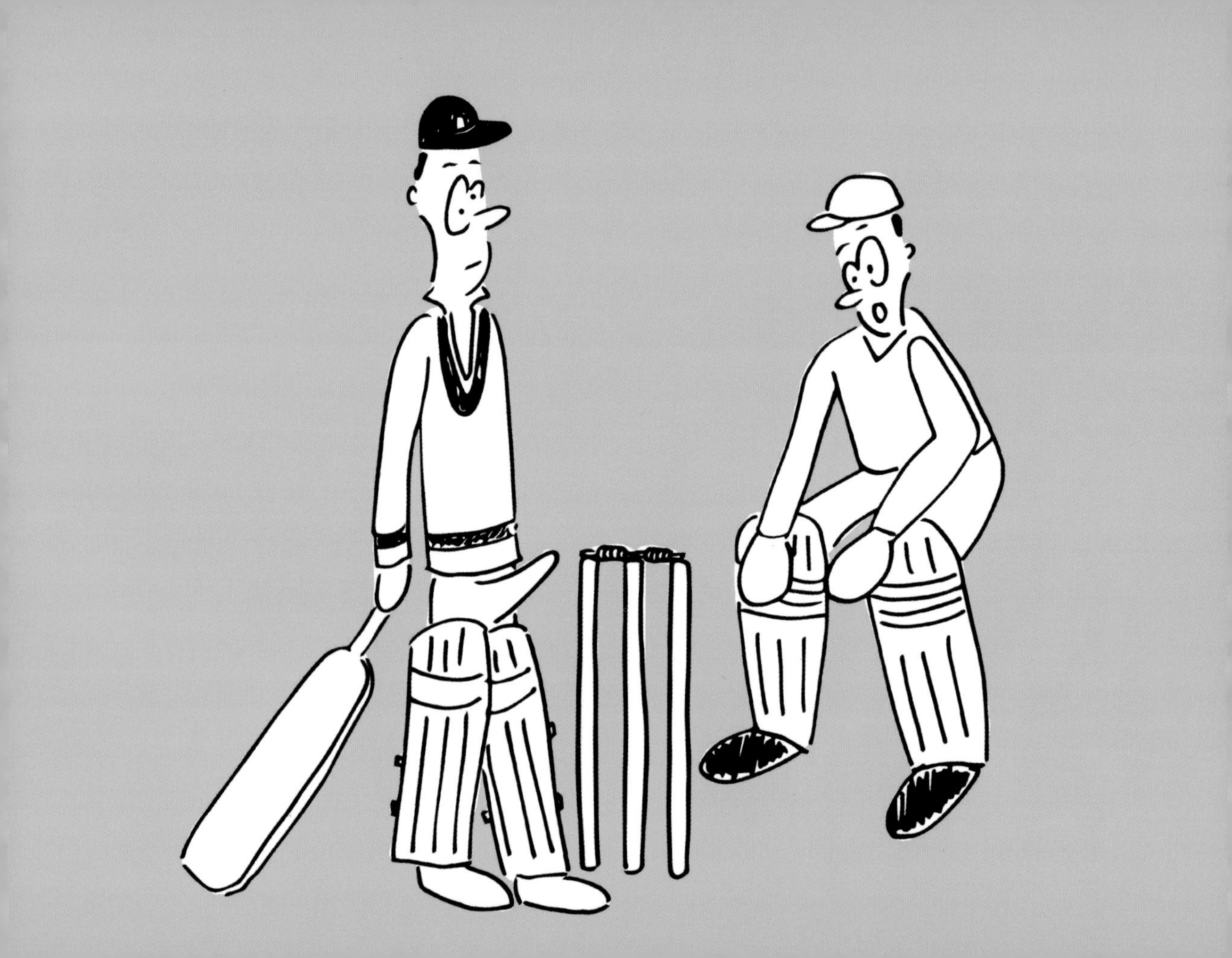

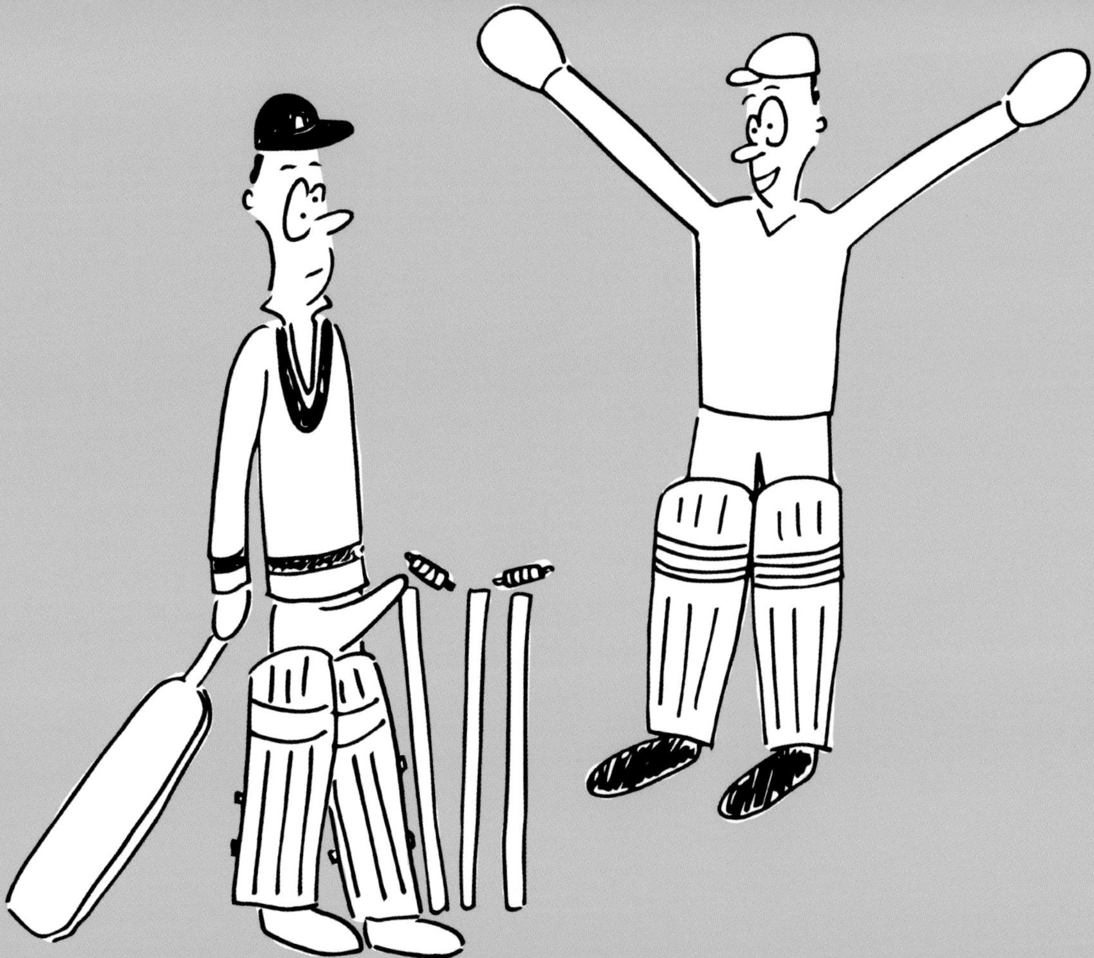

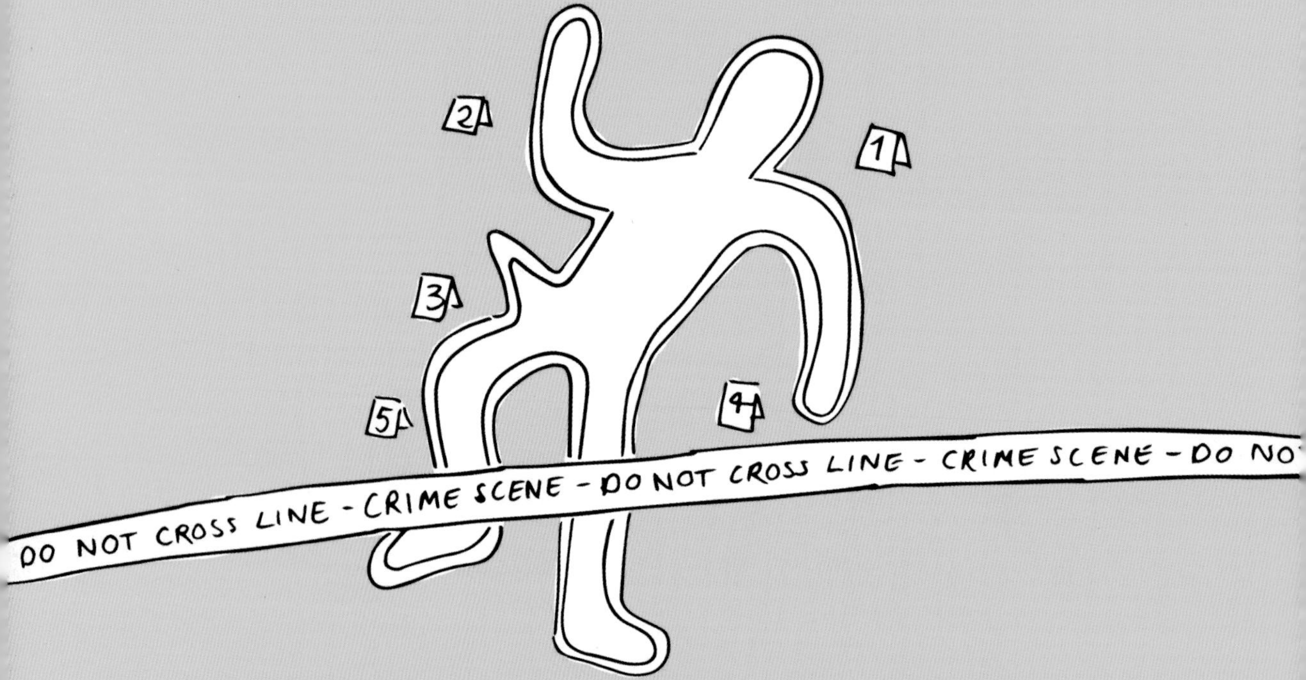
2
1
3
5
4
DO NOT CROSS LINE - CRIME SCENE - DO NOT CROSS LINE - CRIME SCENE - DO NO

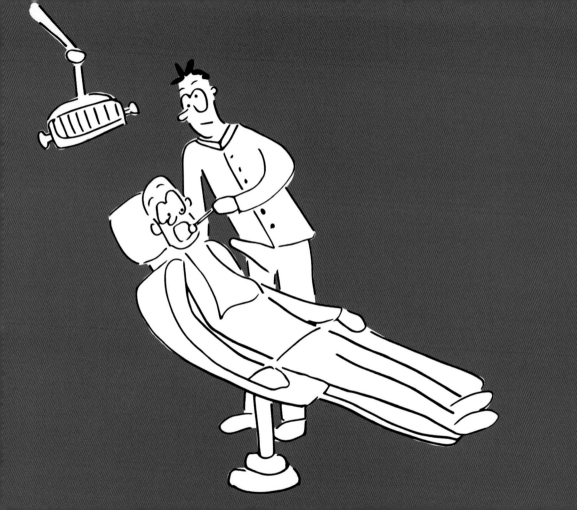

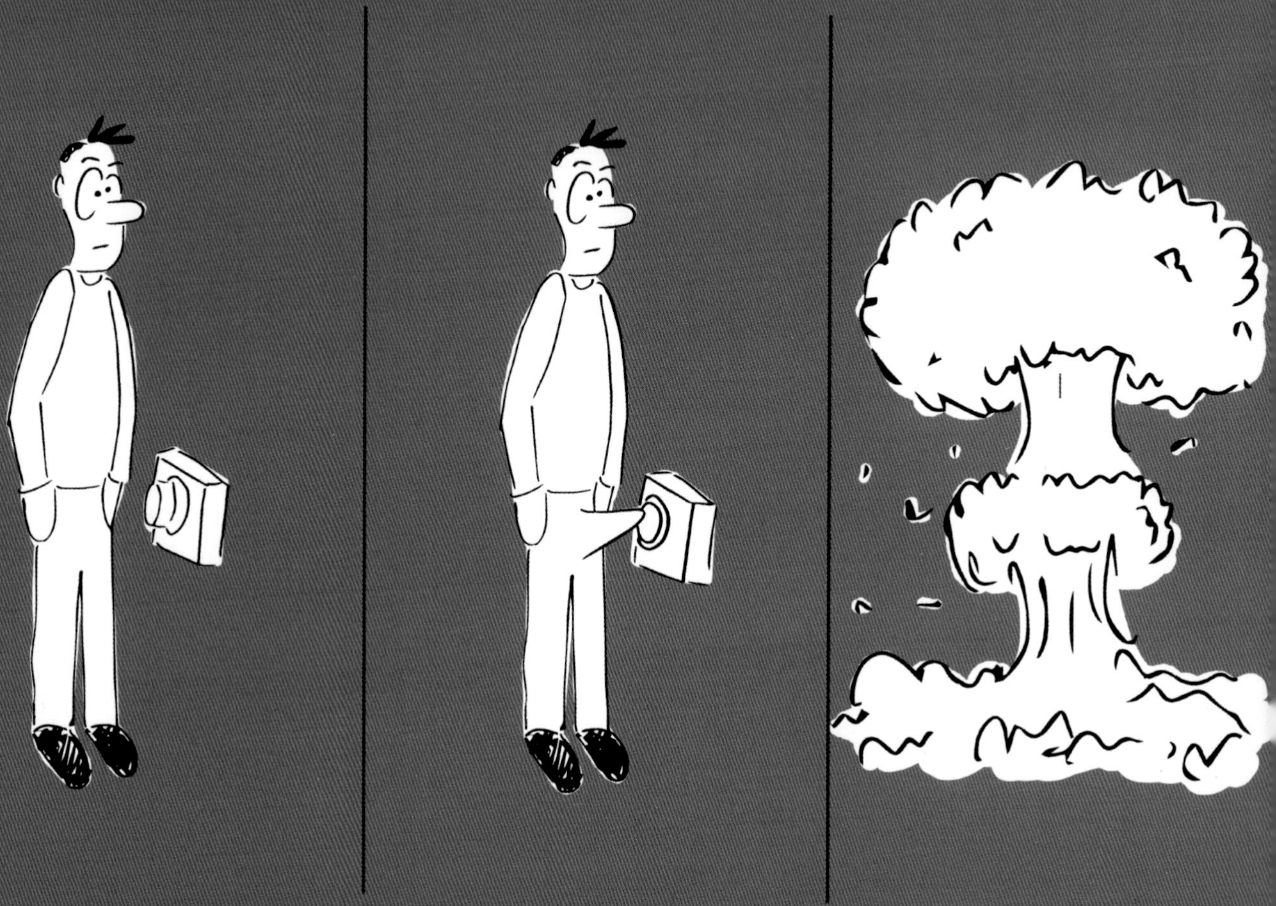

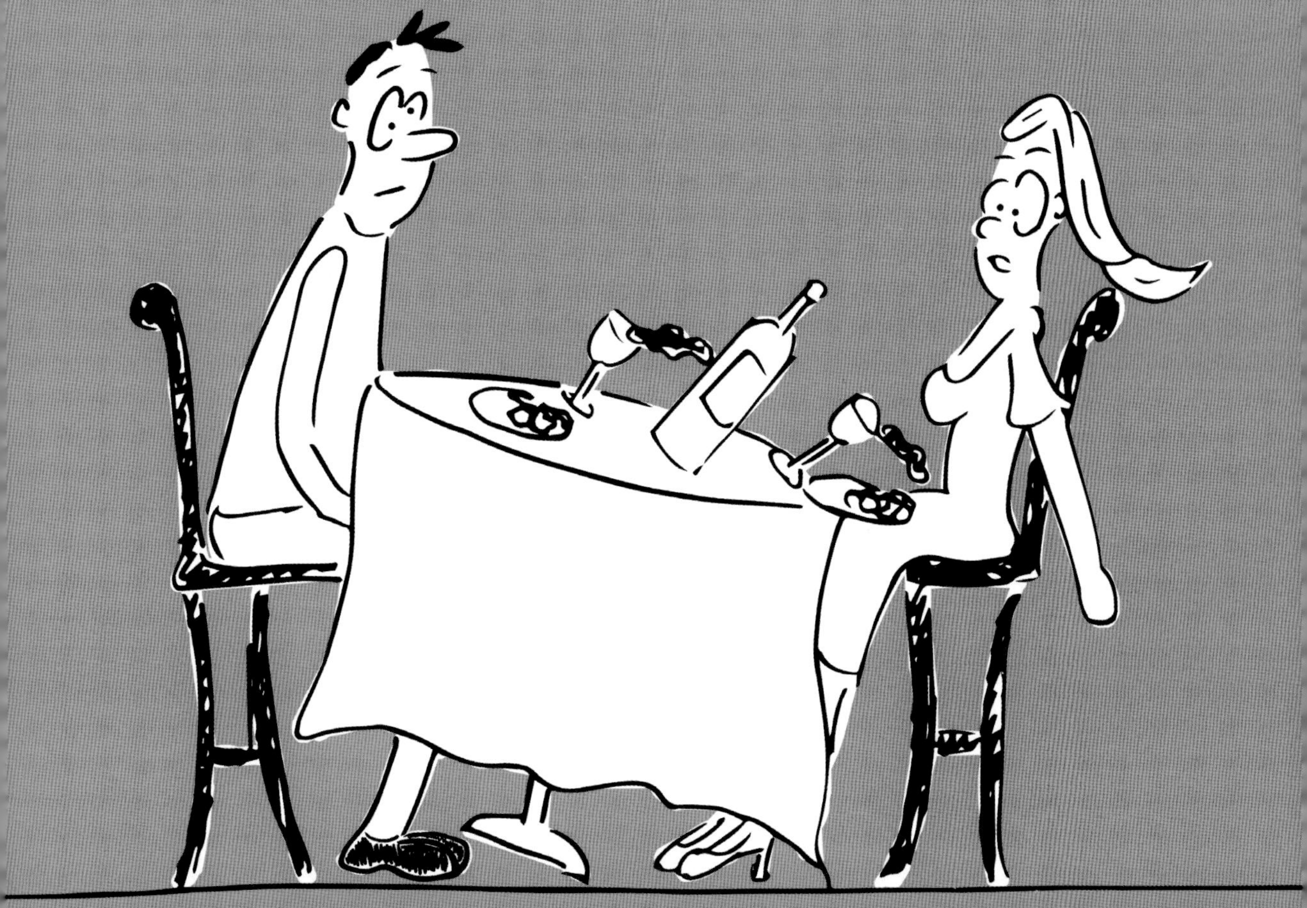

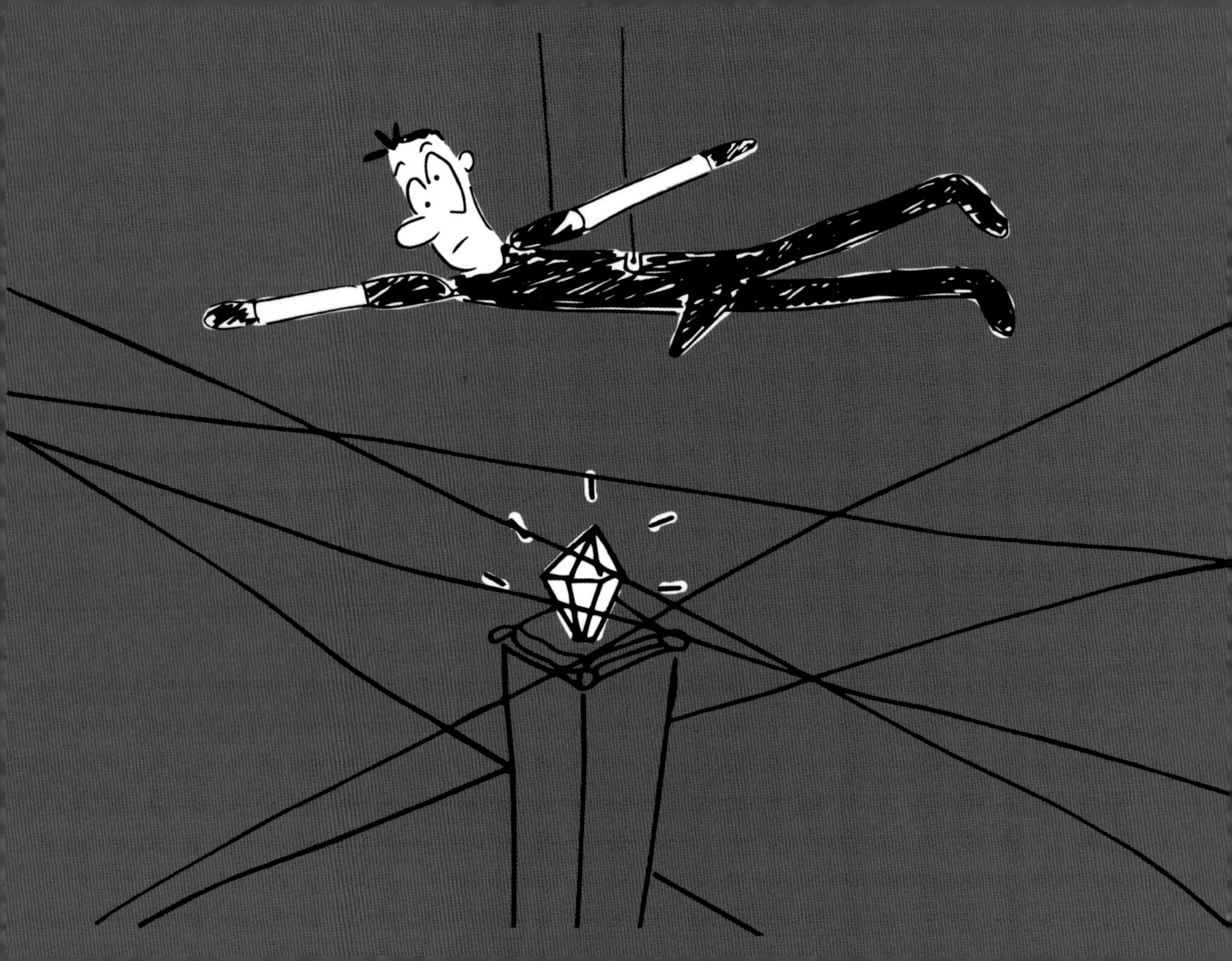

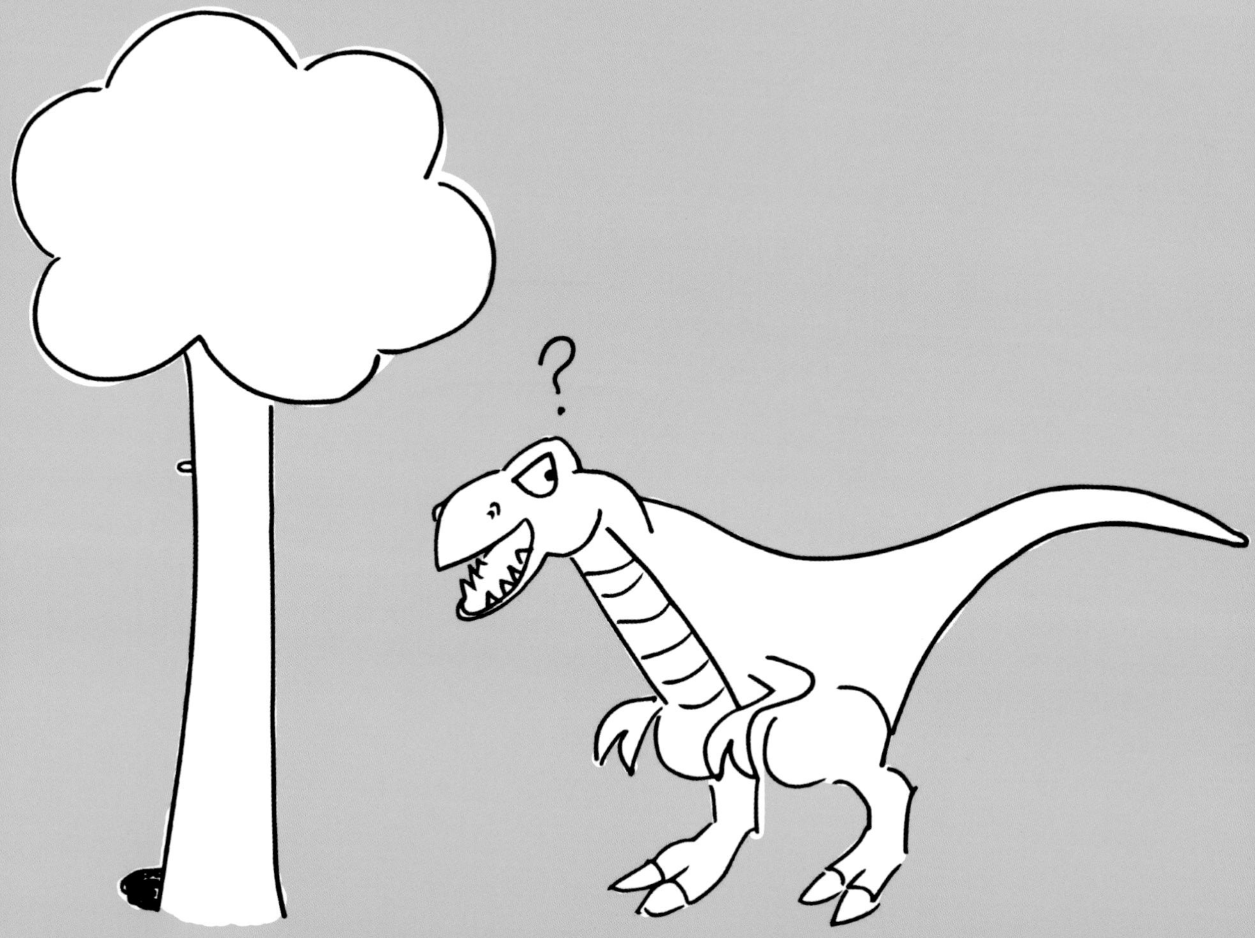

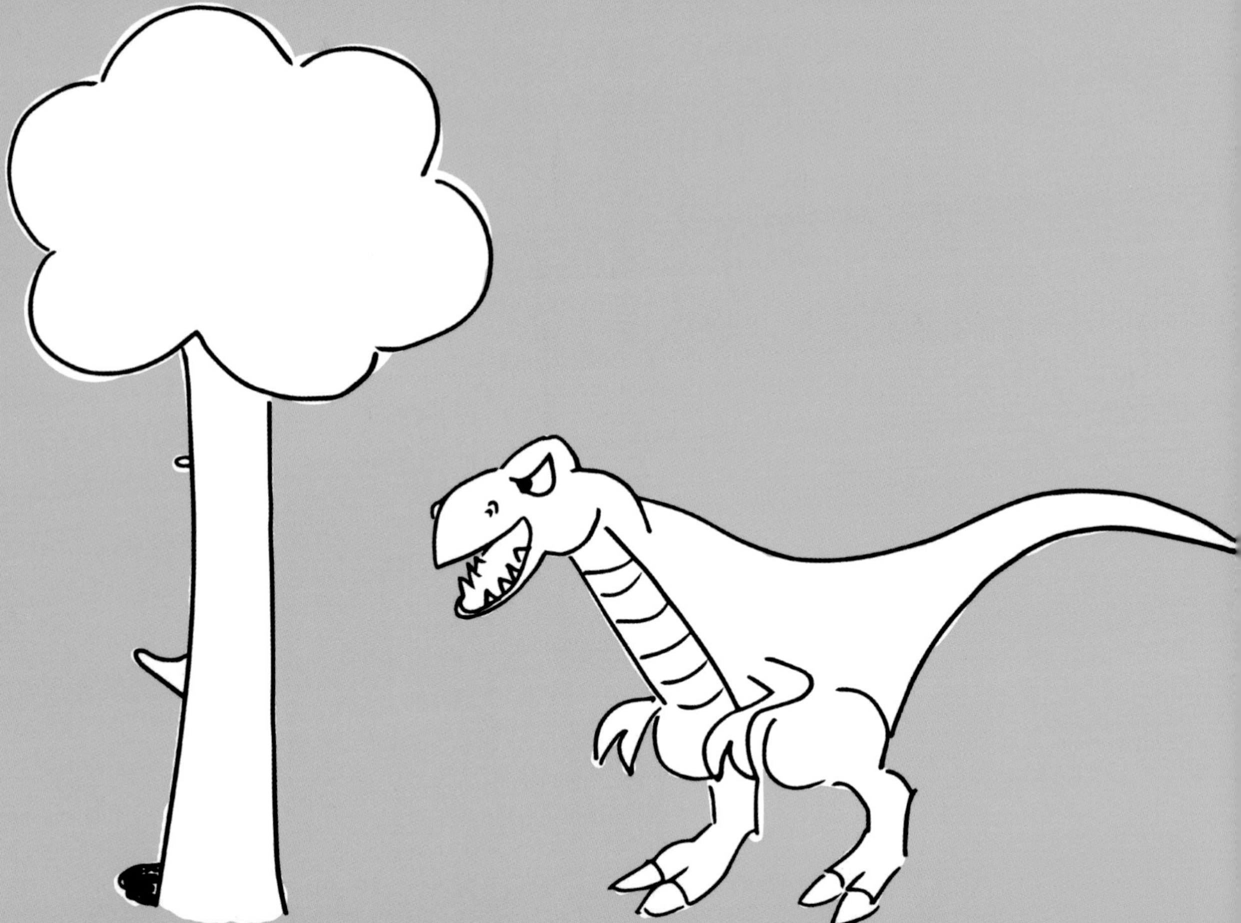

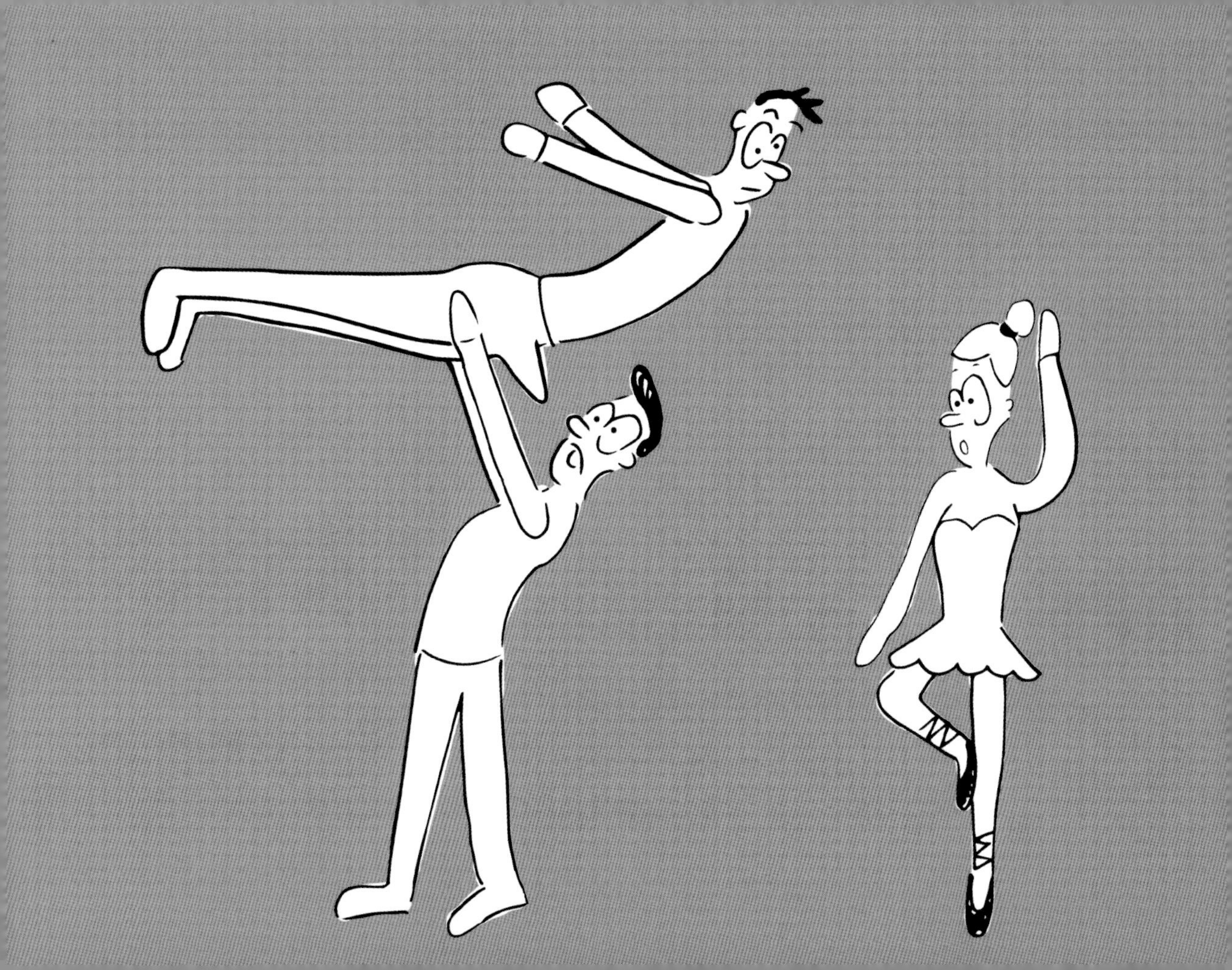

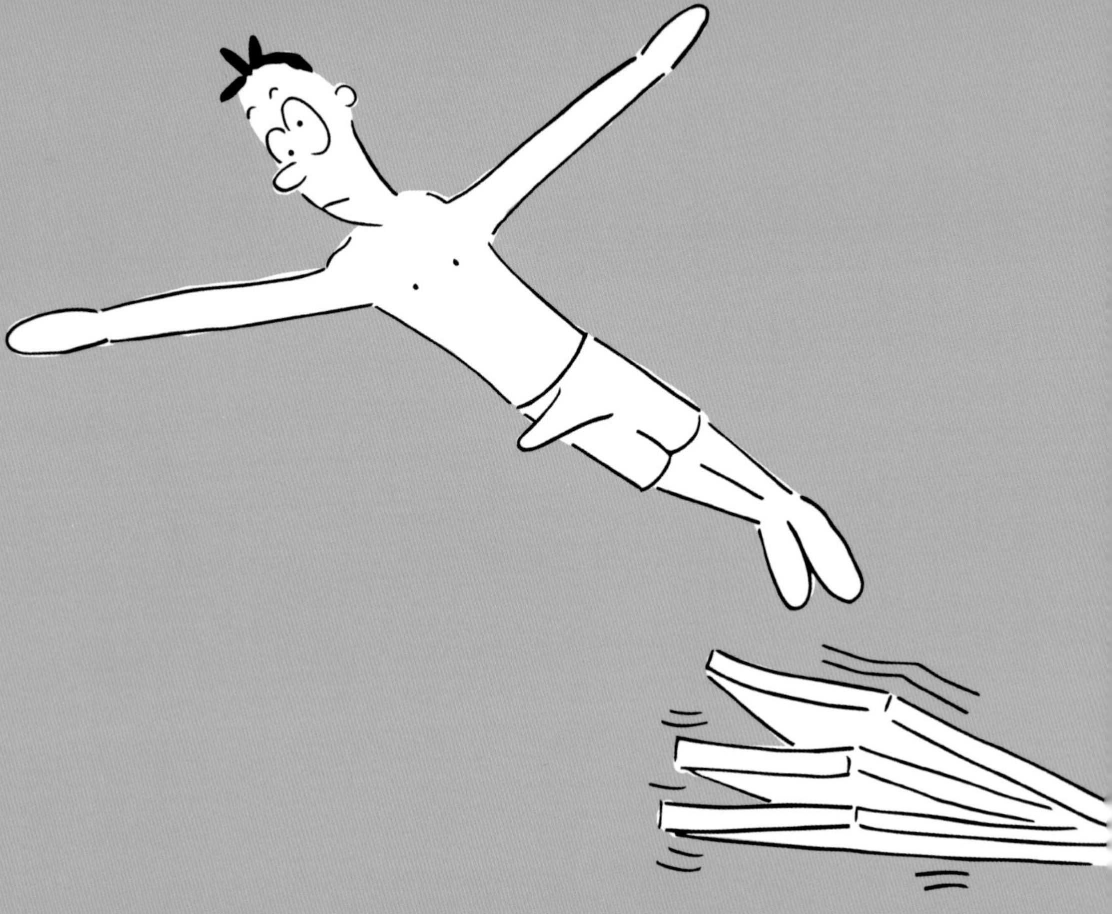

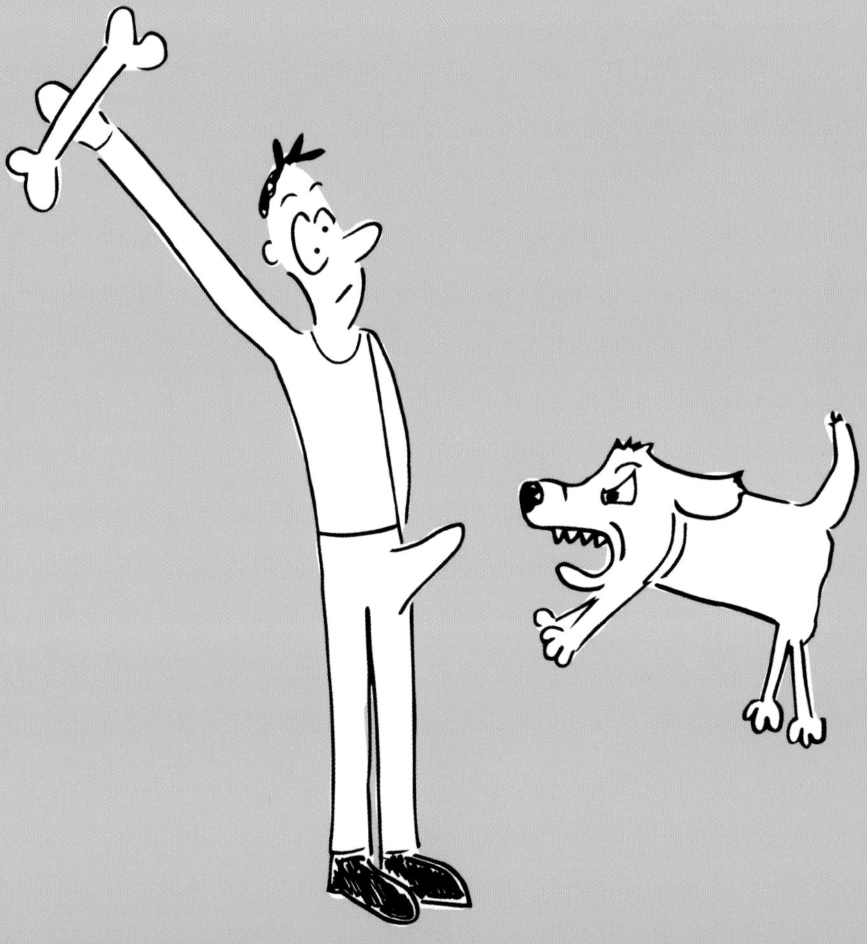

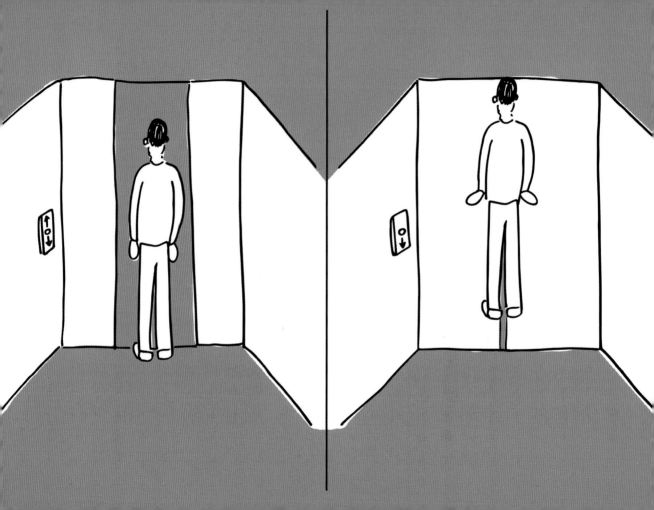

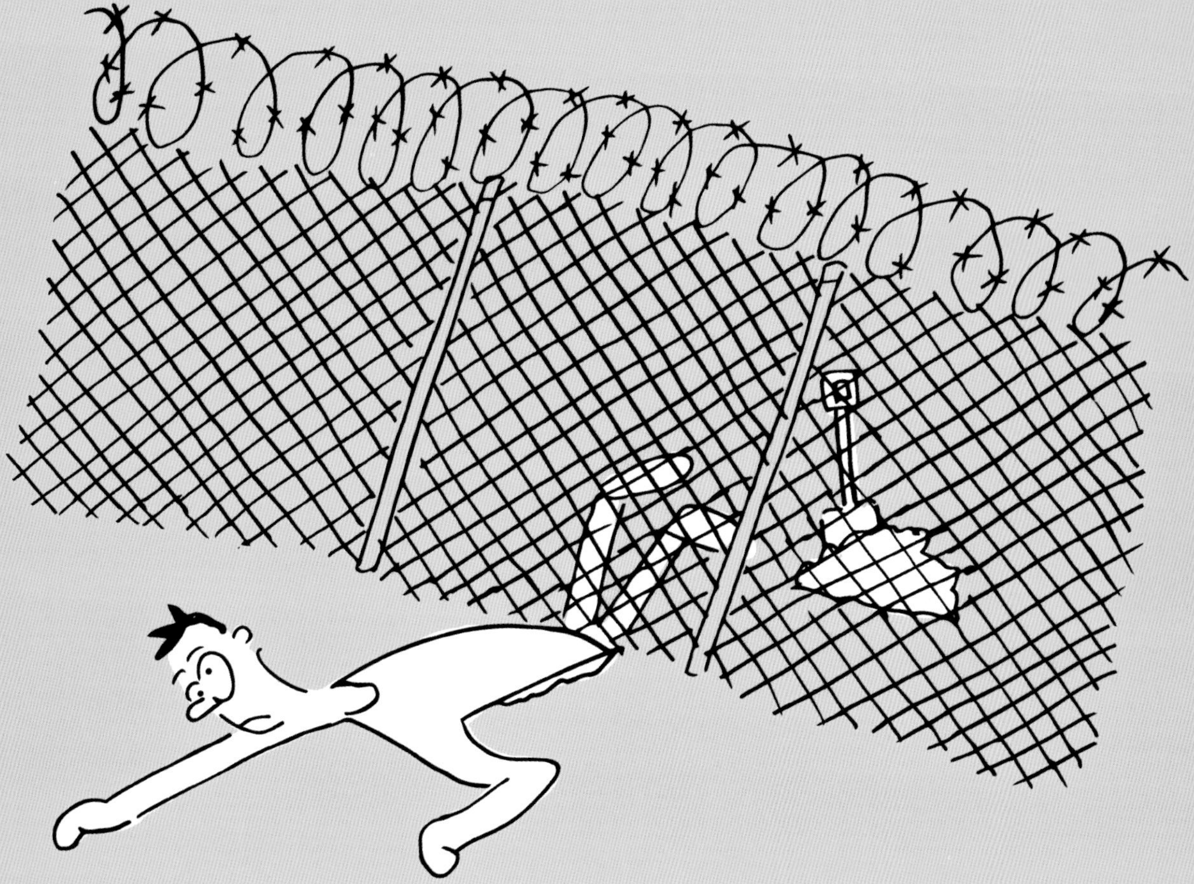

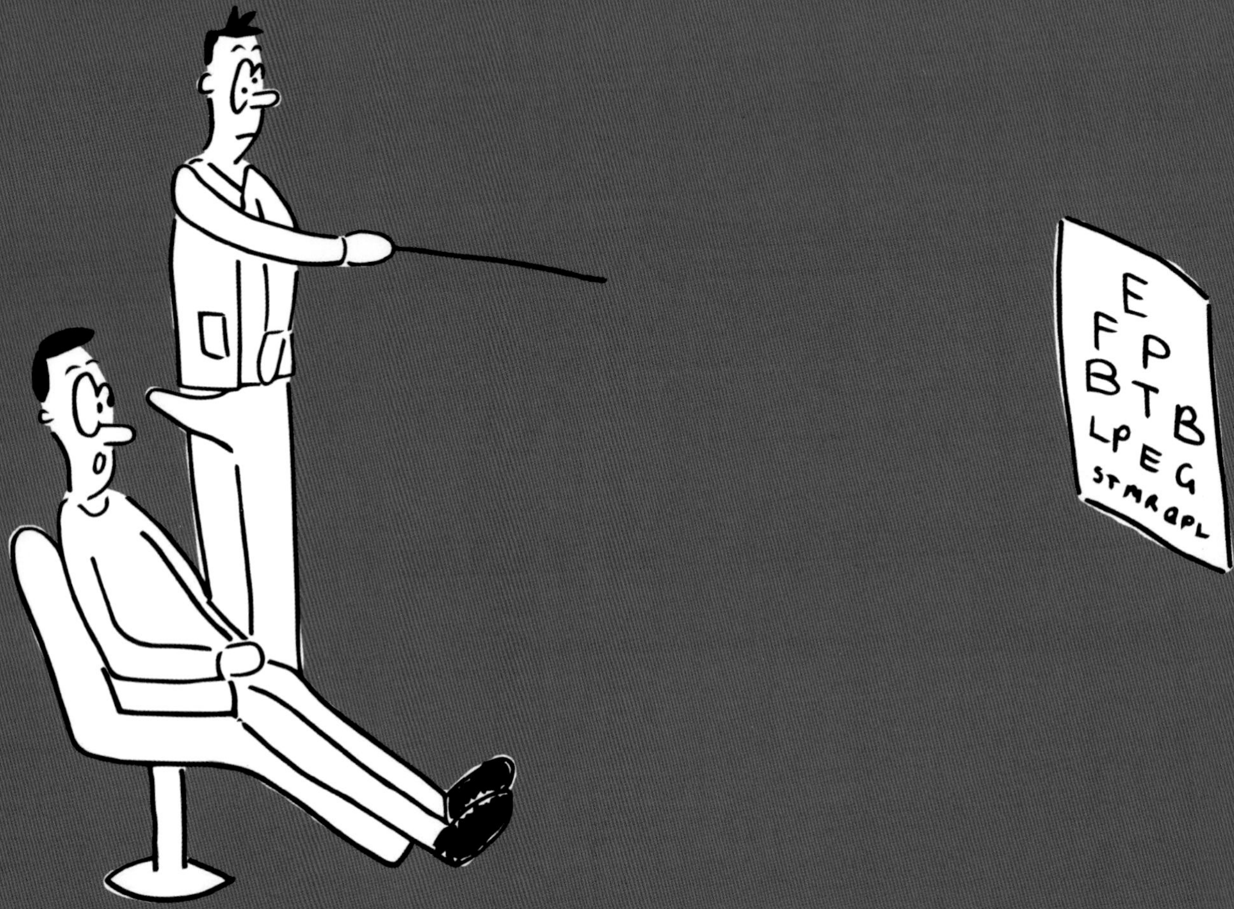
E
F P
B T B
LP E G
STMRQPL

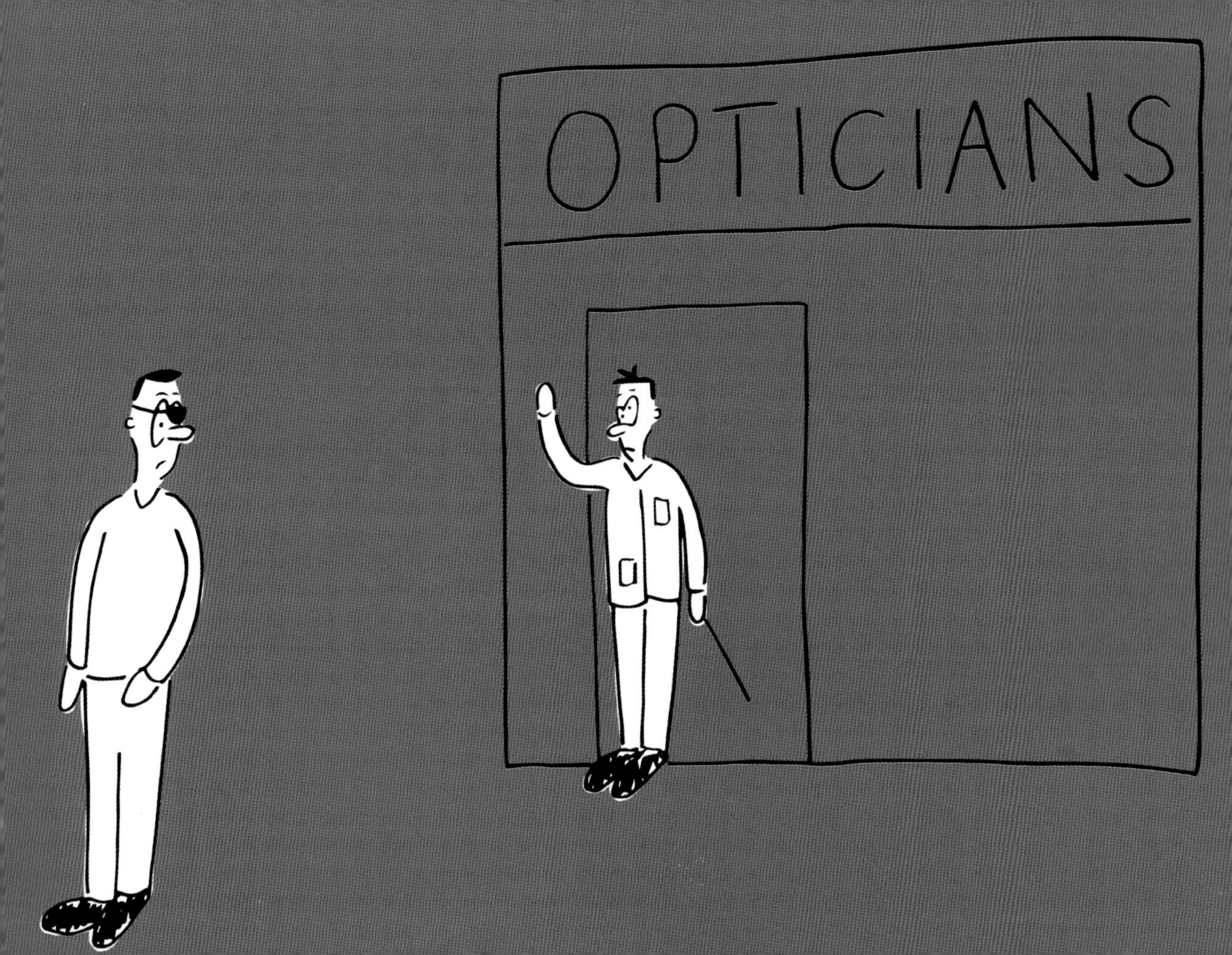
OPTICIANS

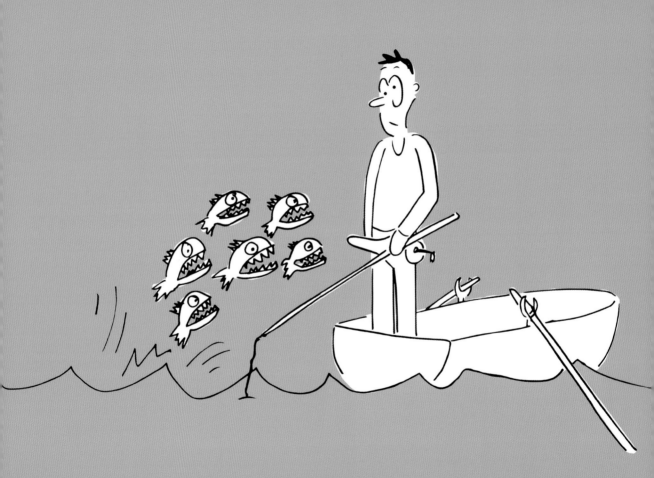

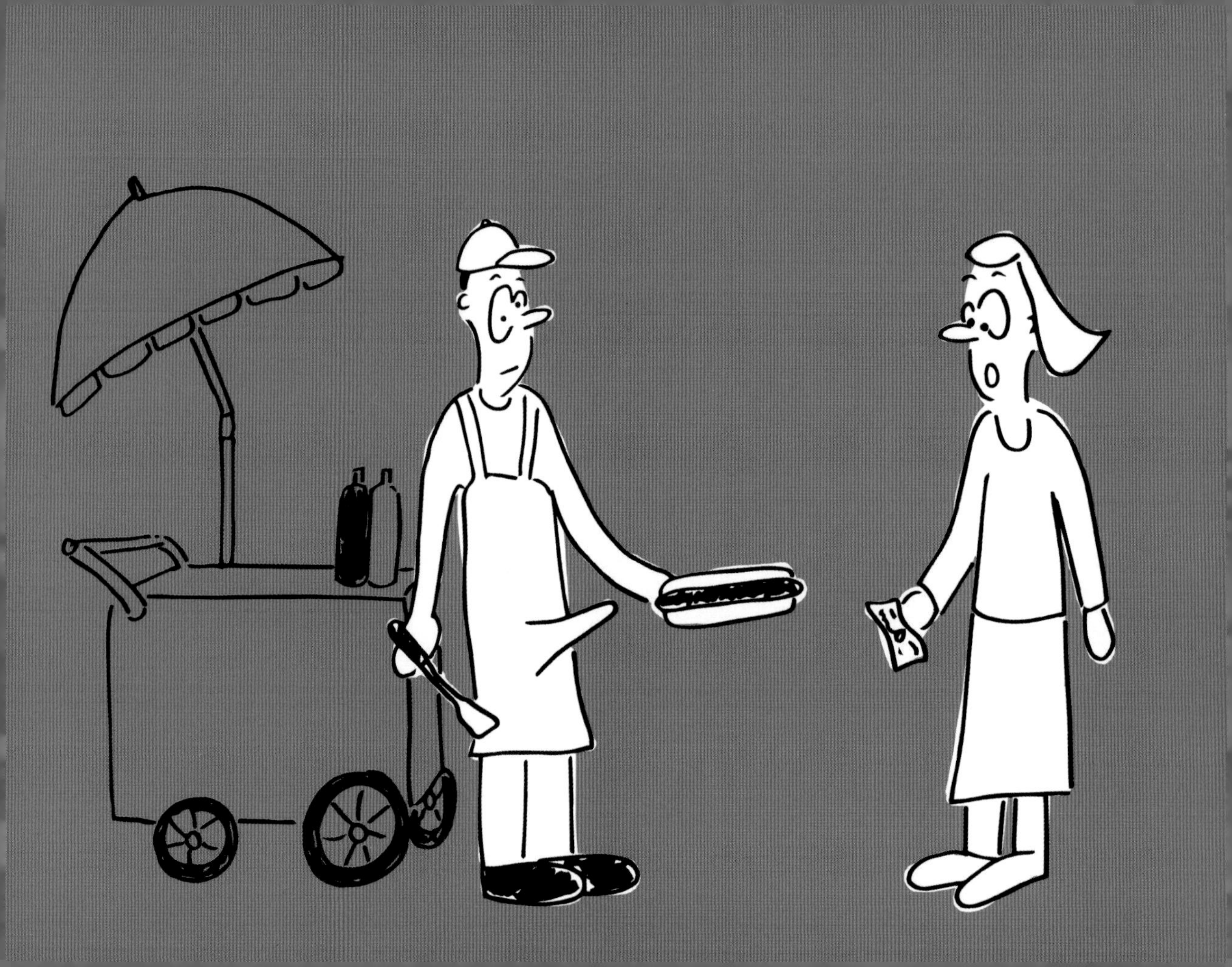

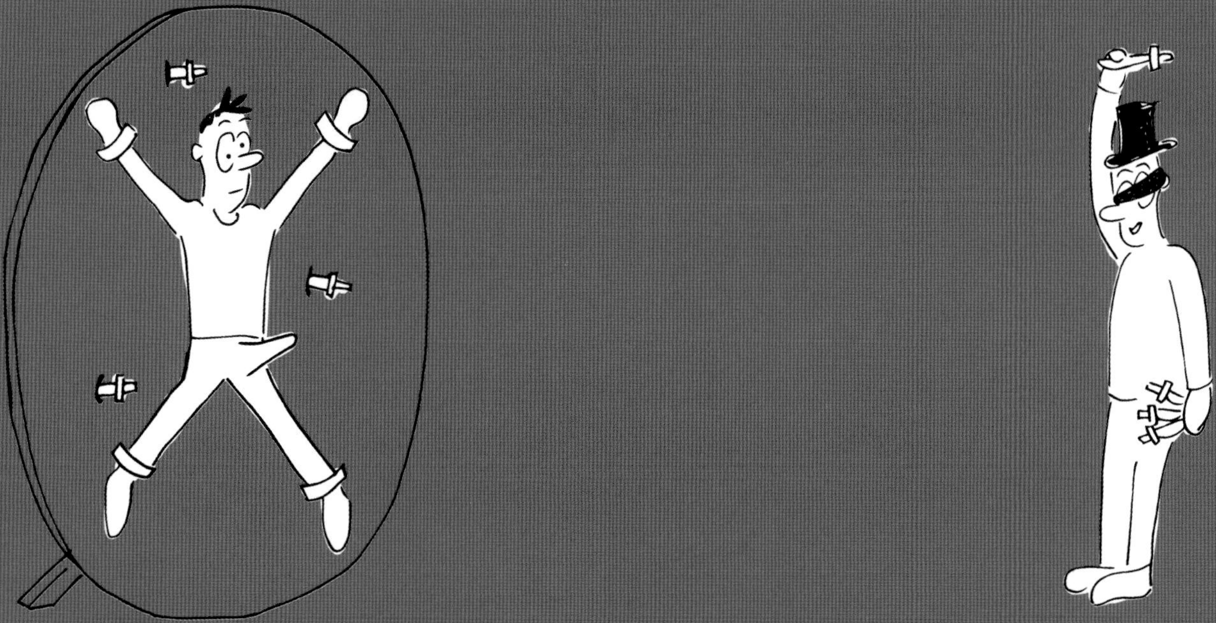

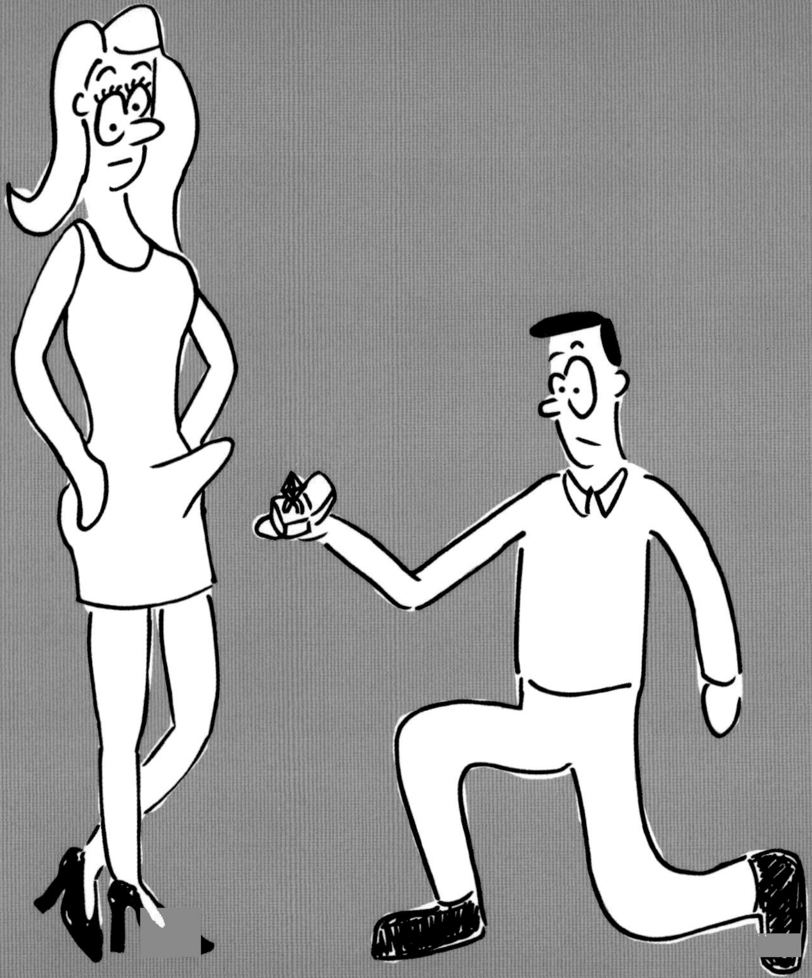

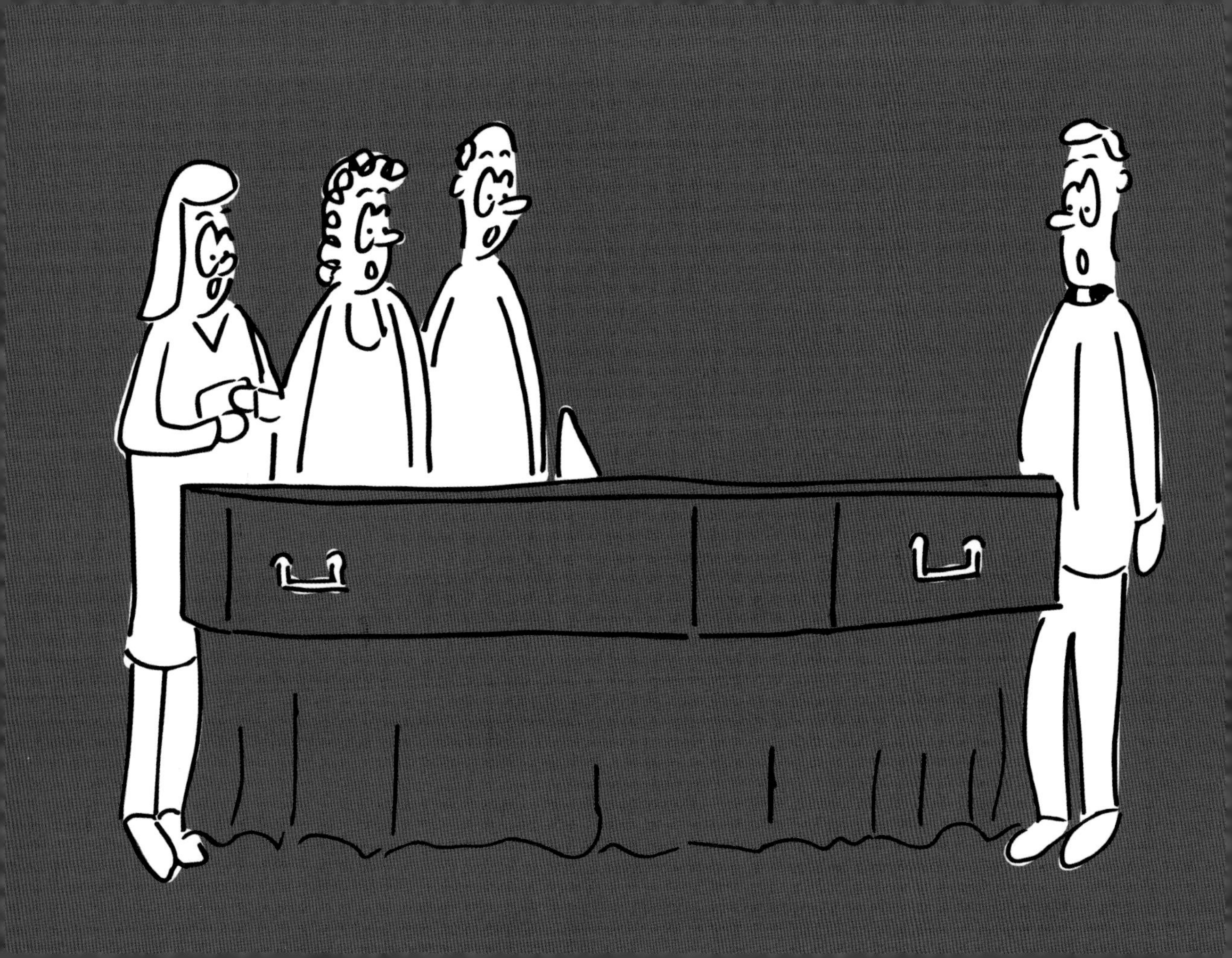

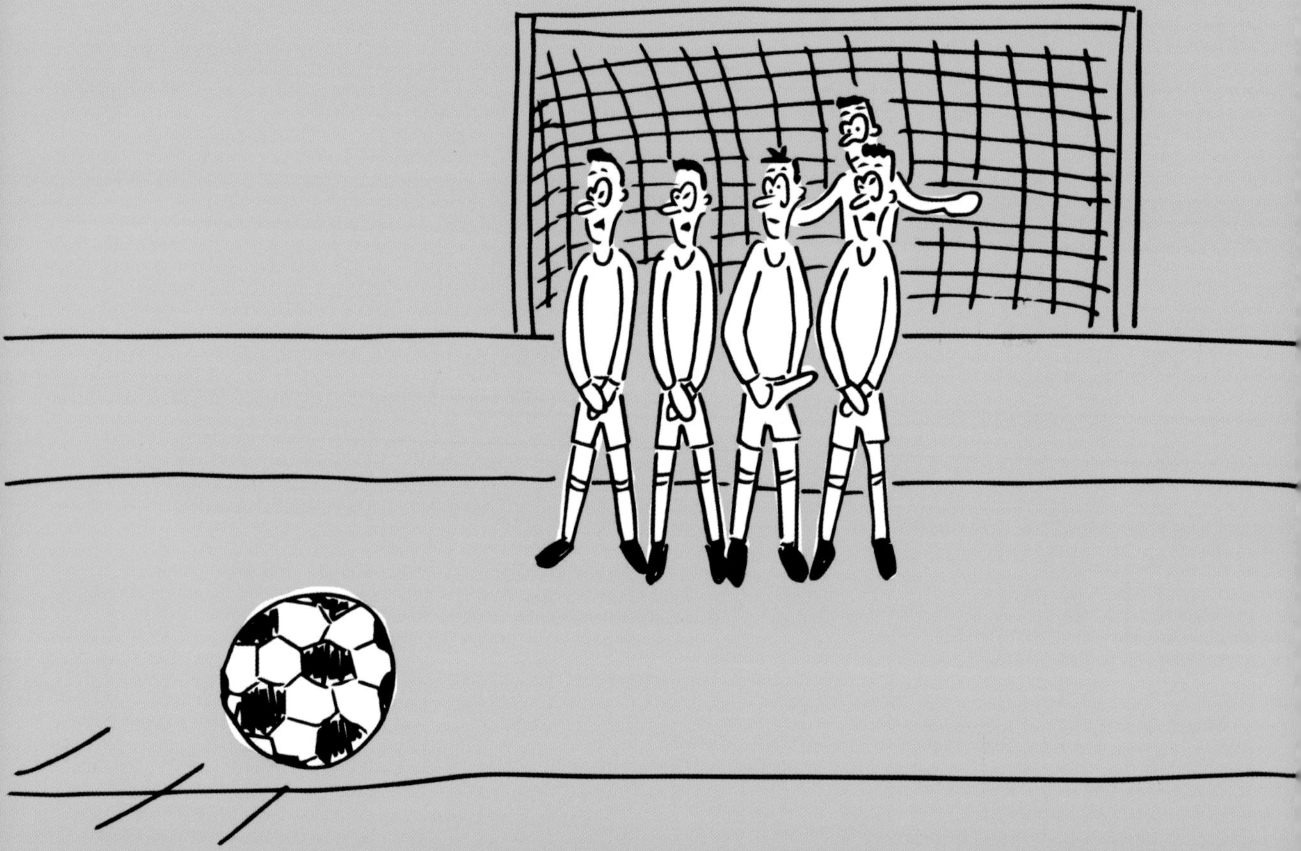

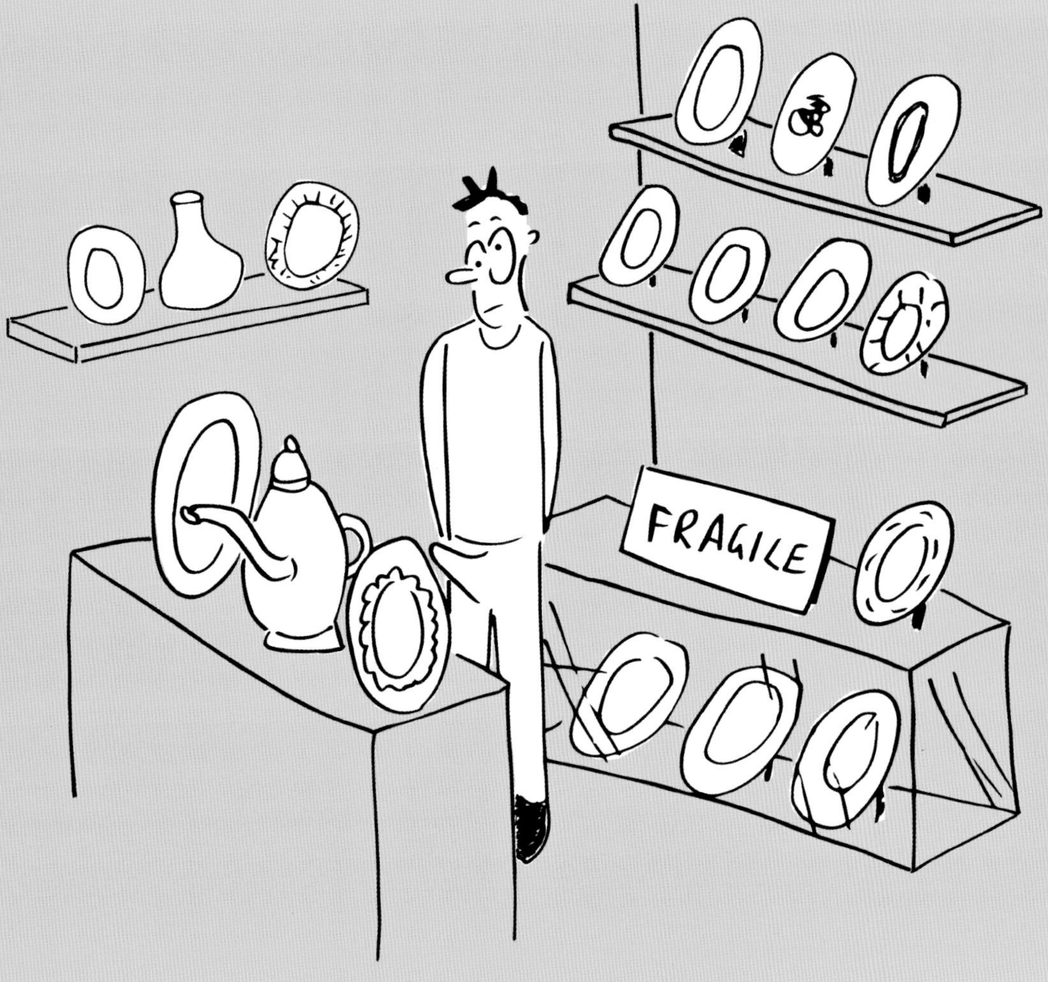
FRAGILE

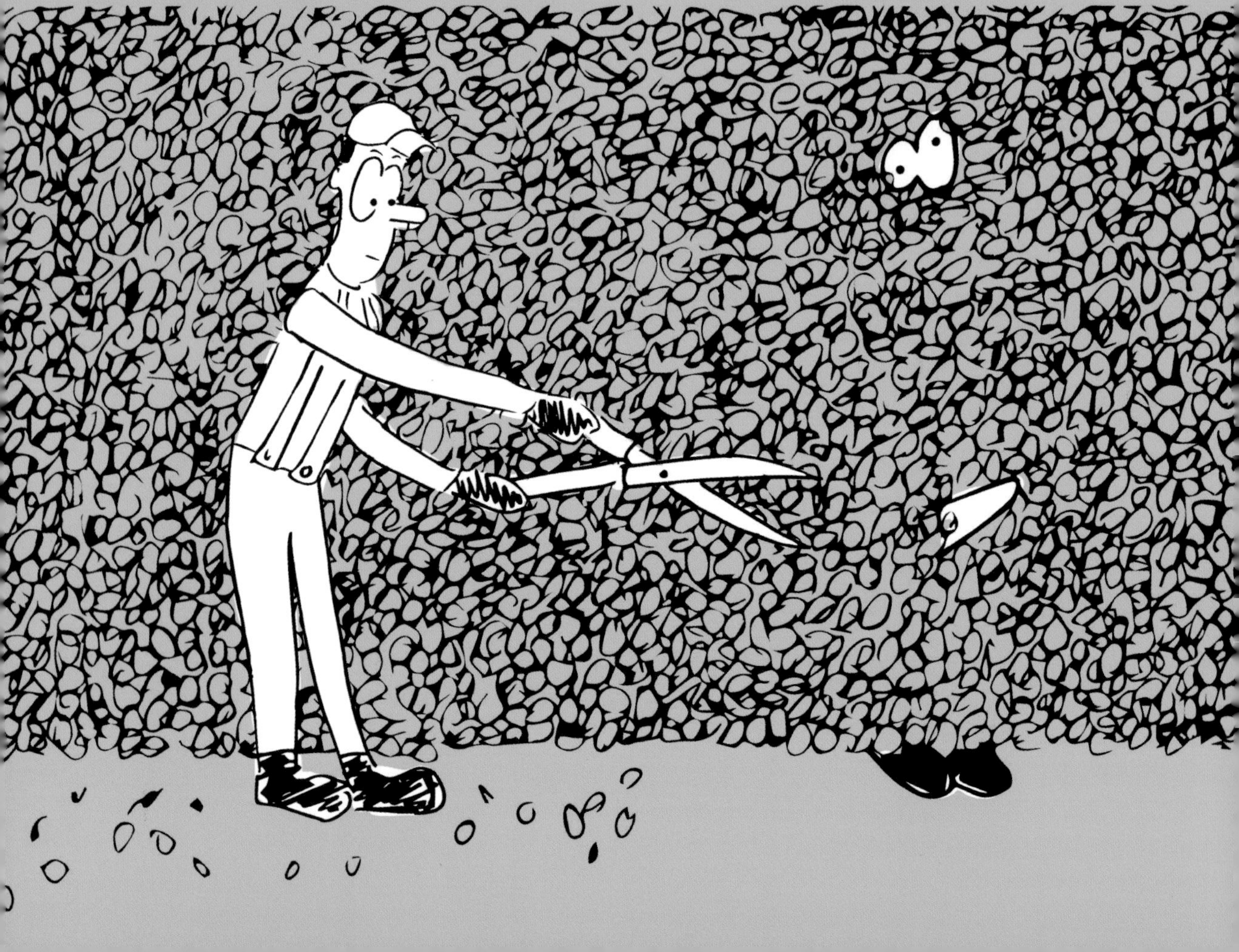

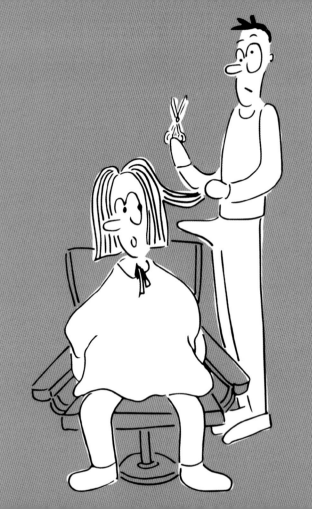

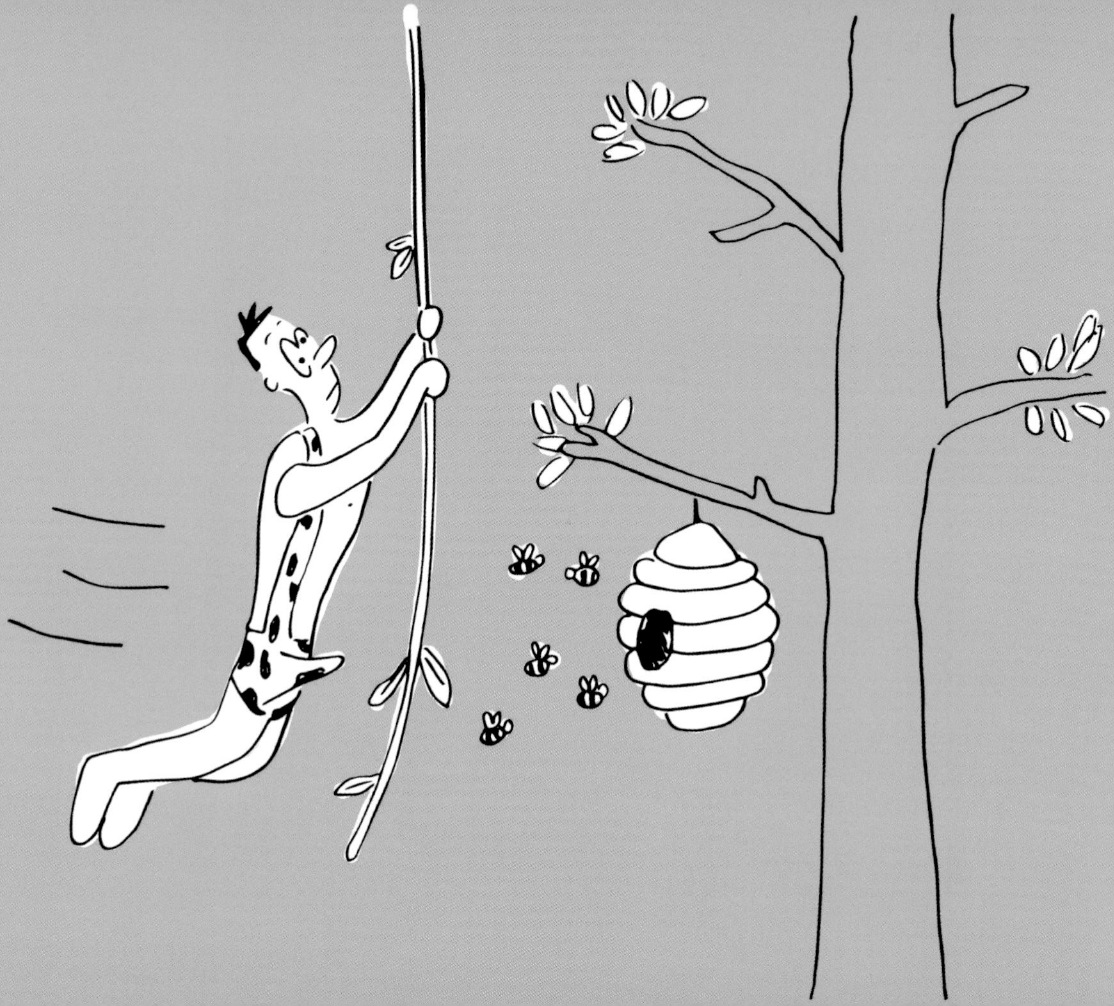

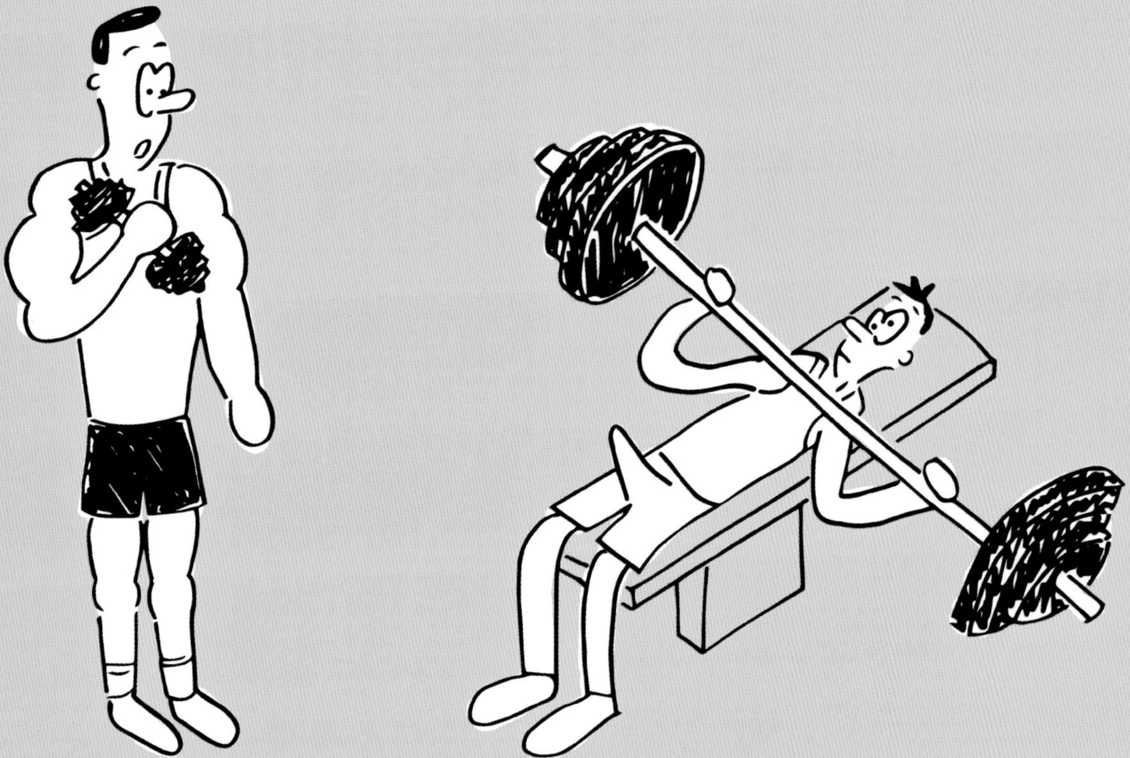

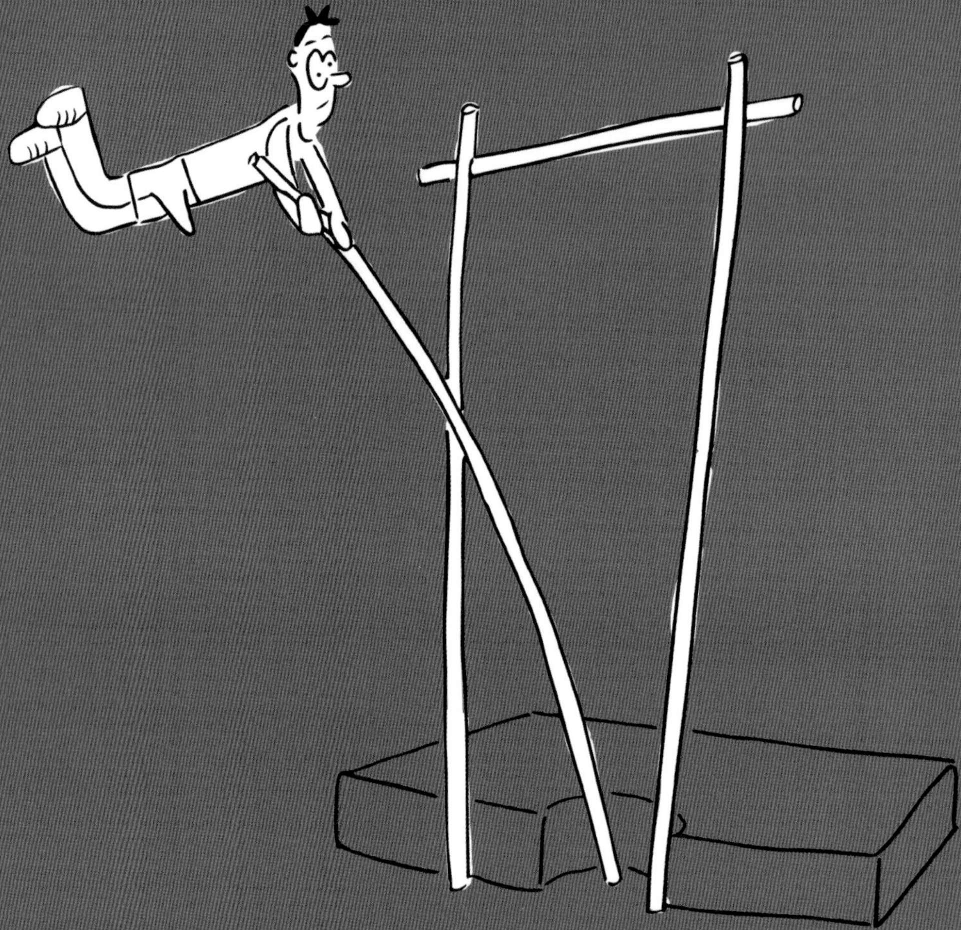

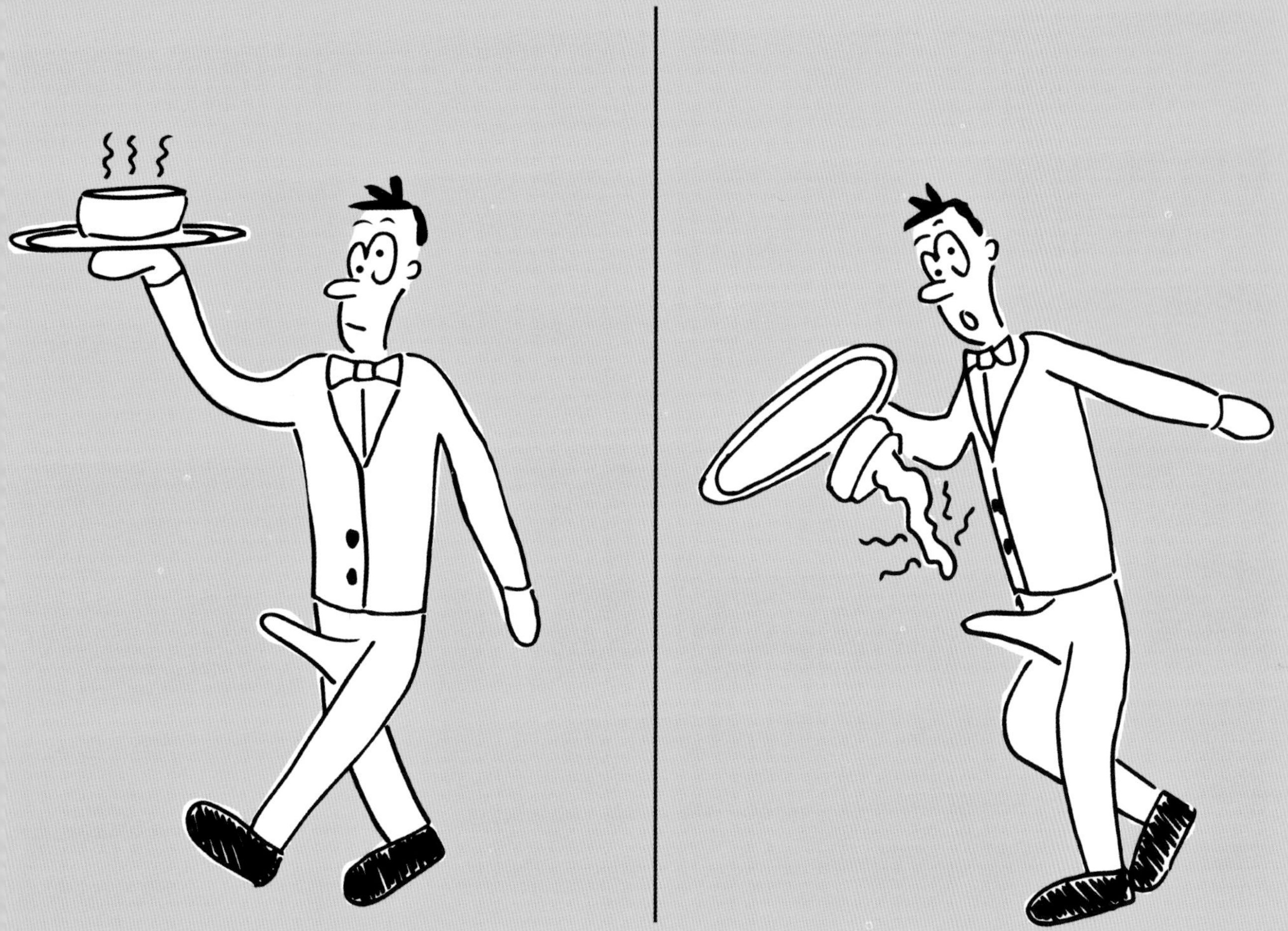

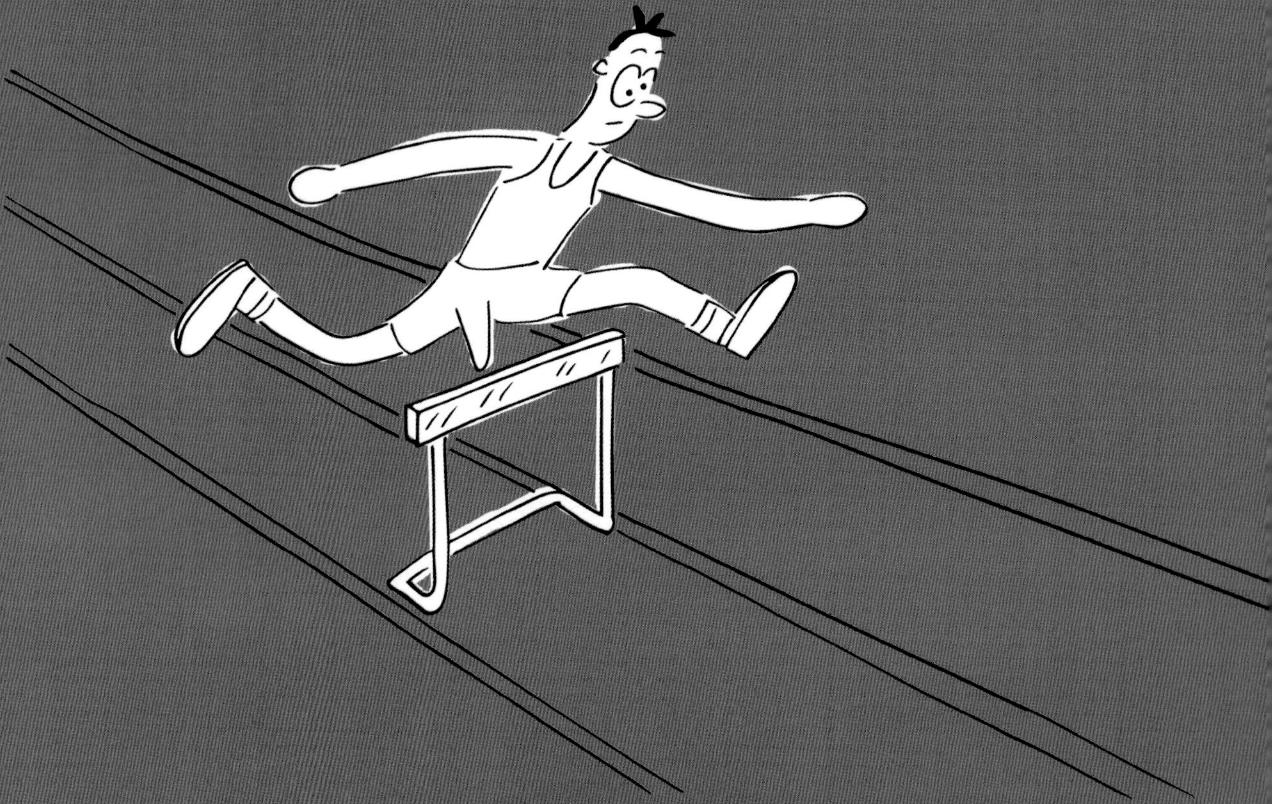

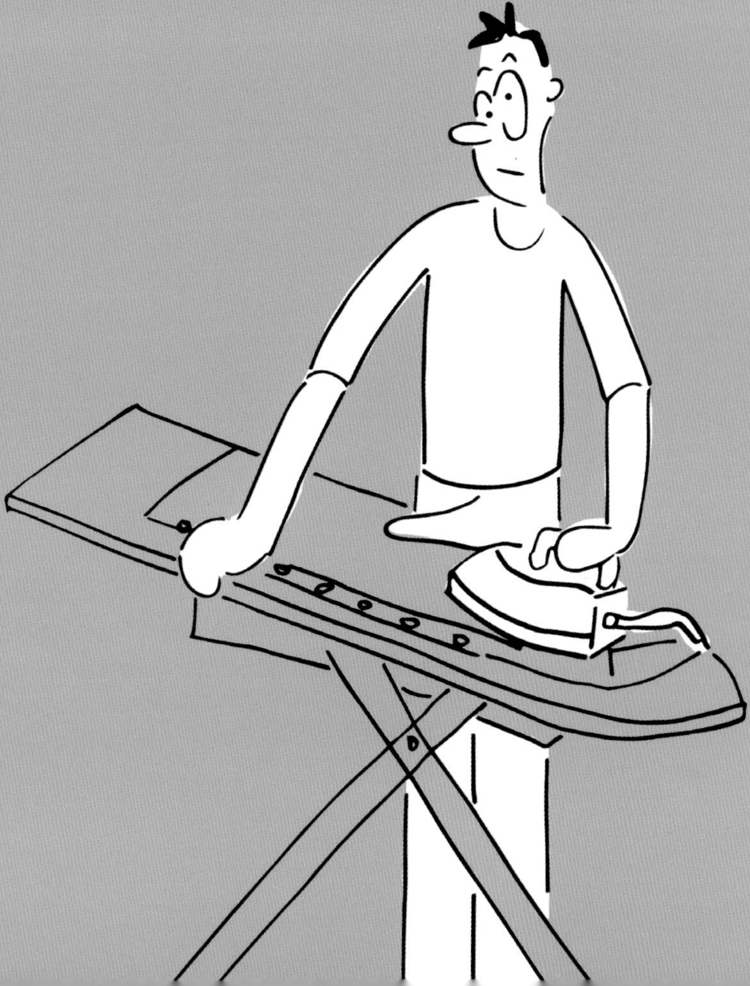

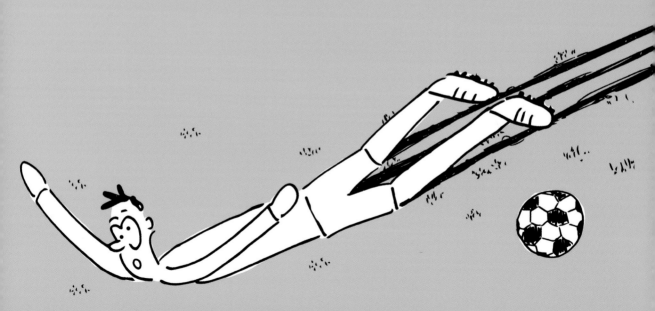

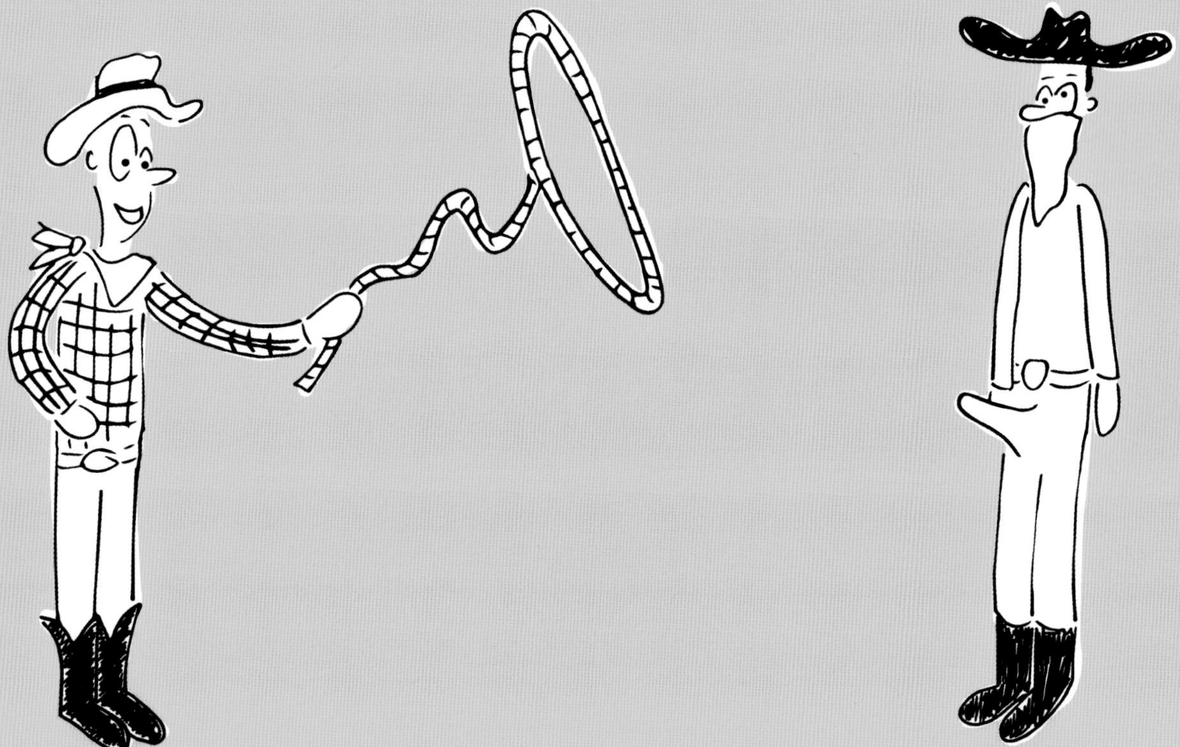

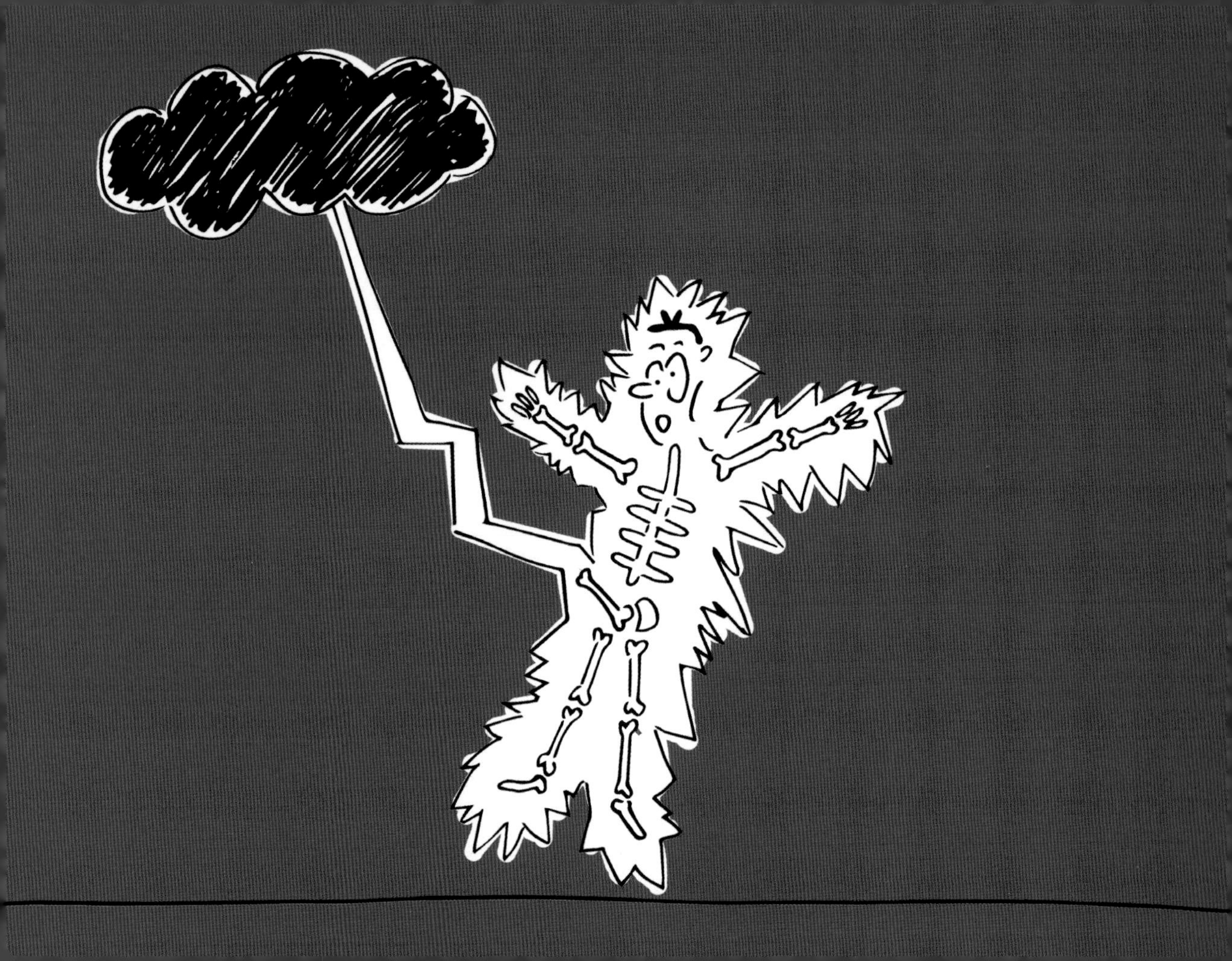

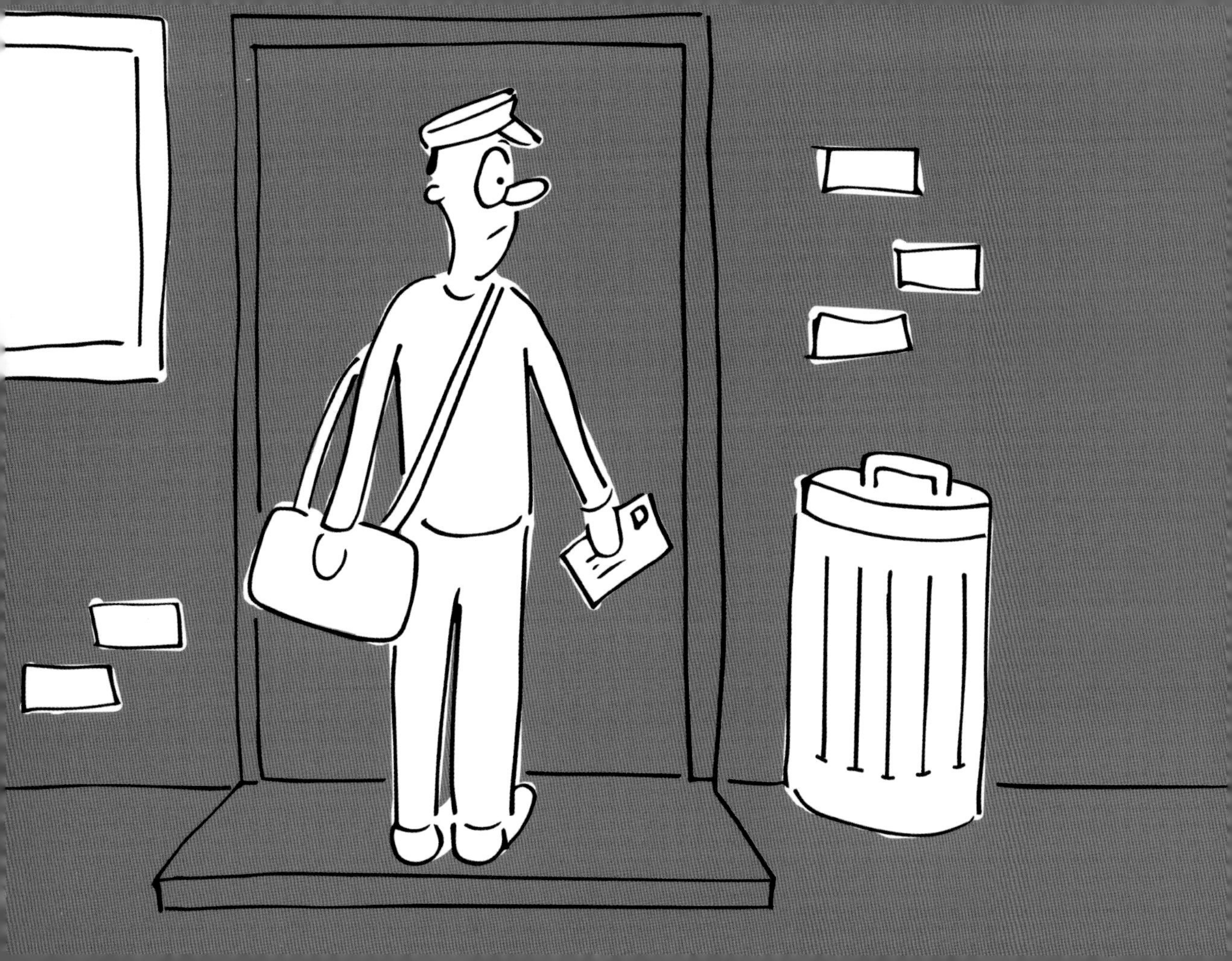

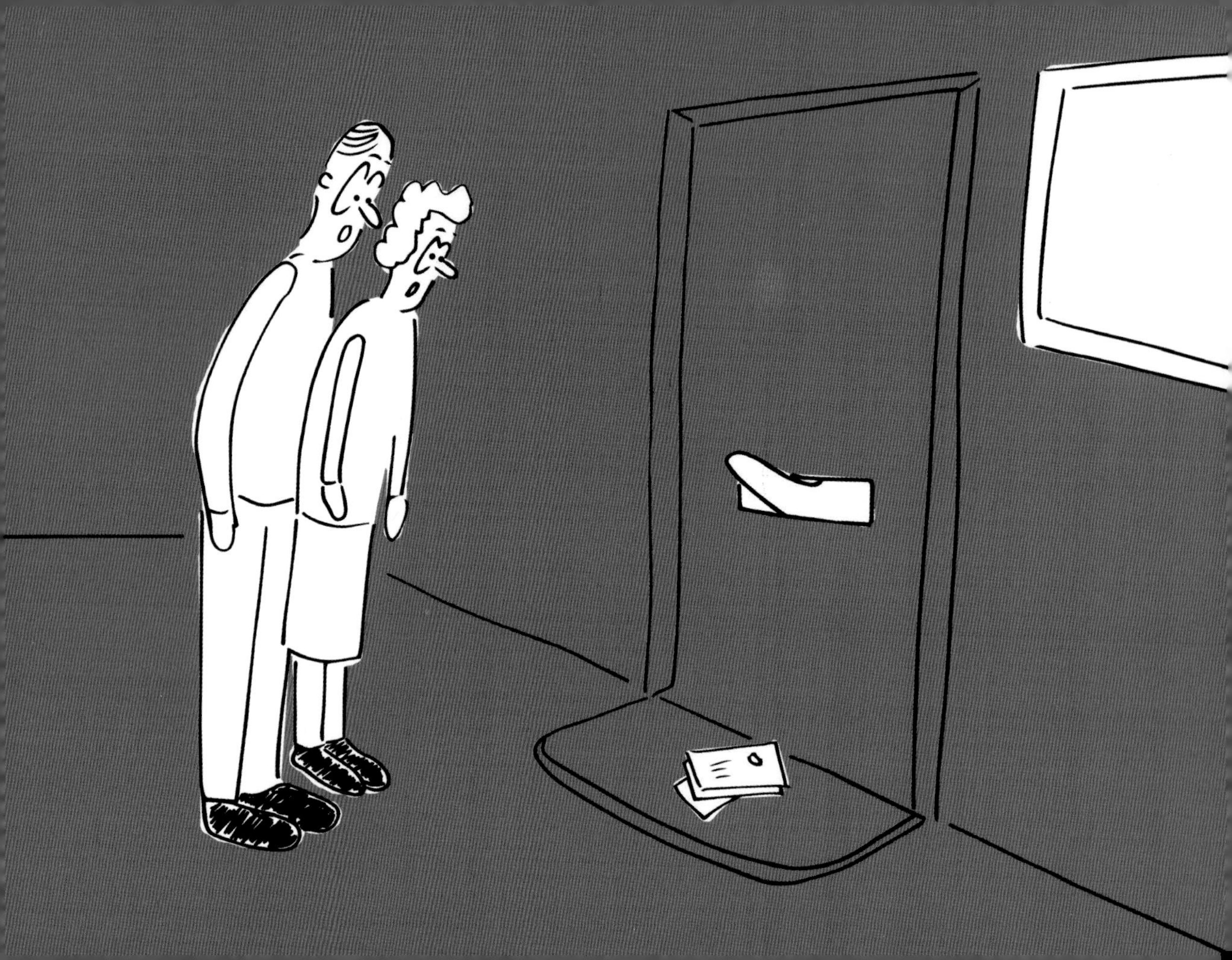

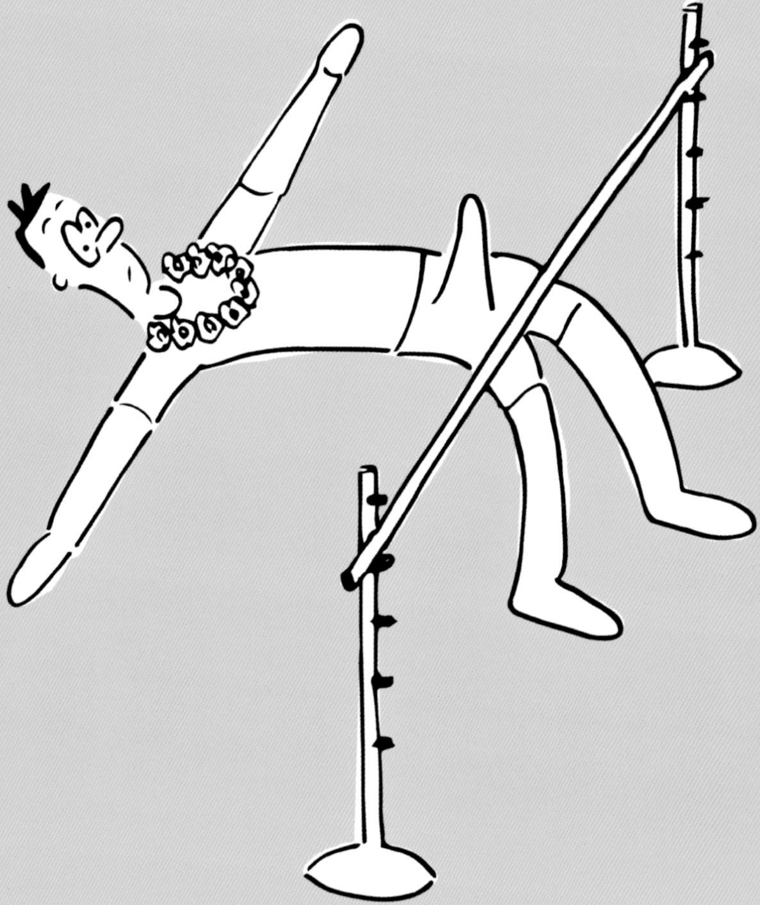

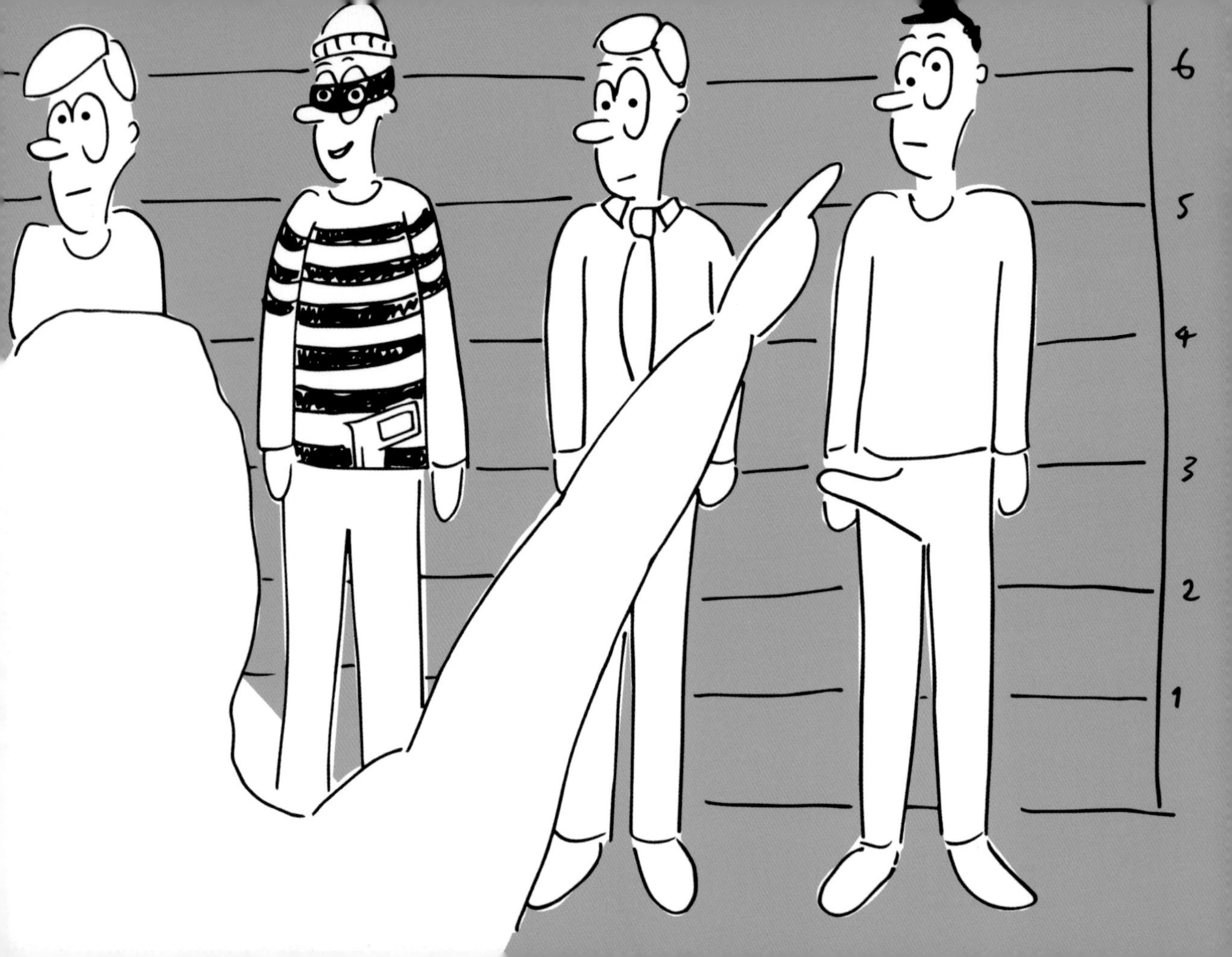
6
5
4
3
2
1

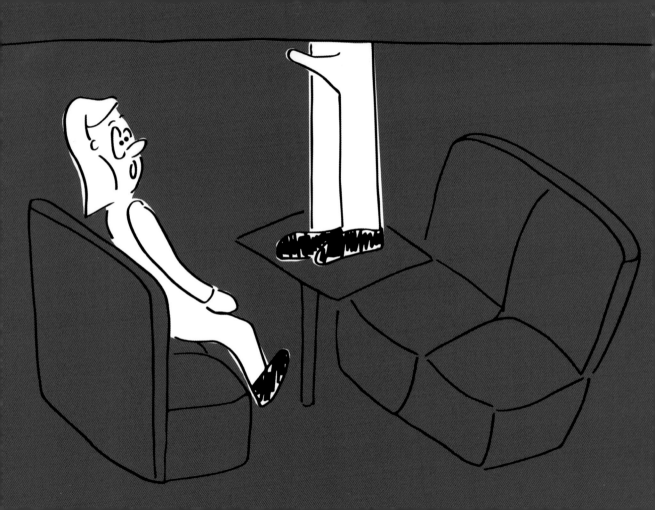

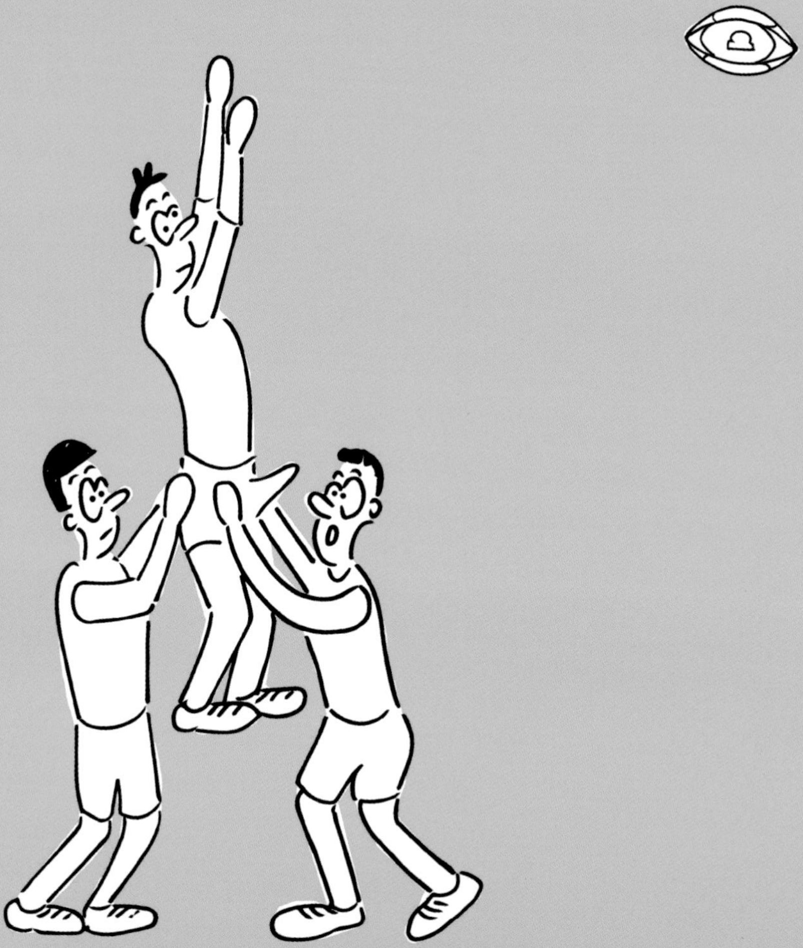

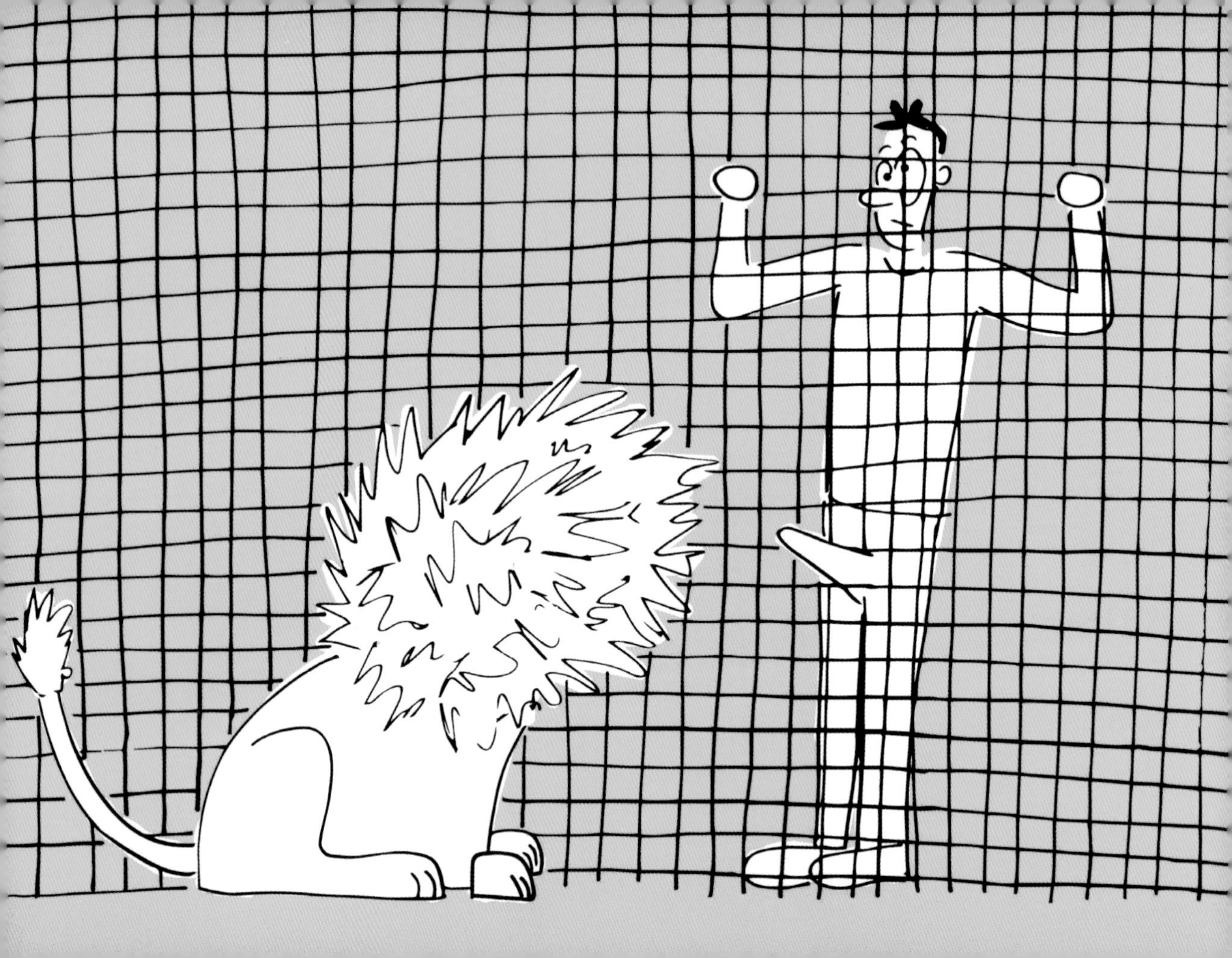

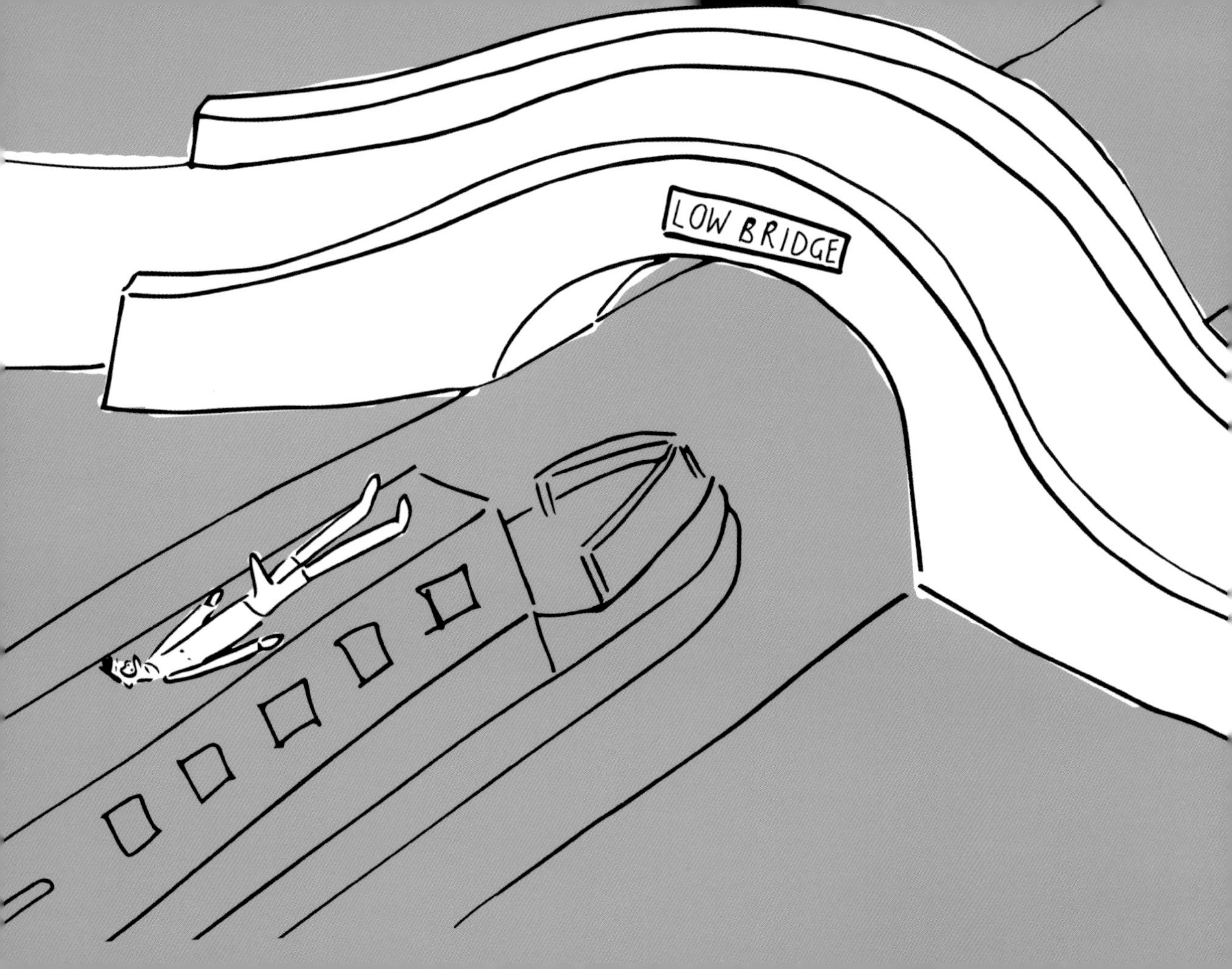
LOW BRIDGE

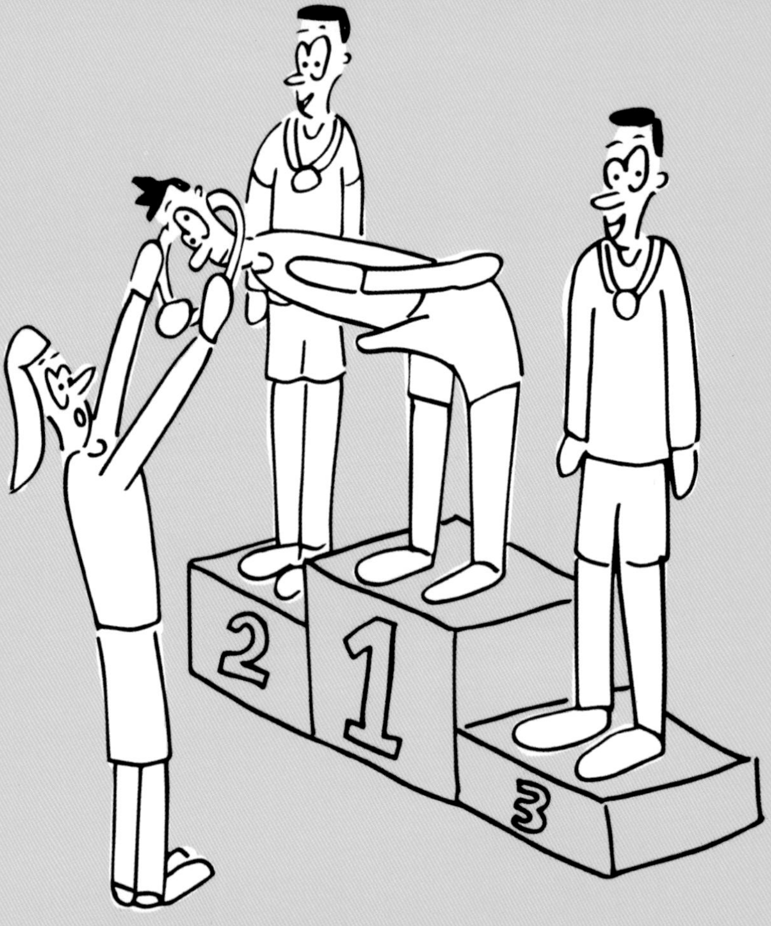
2
1
3

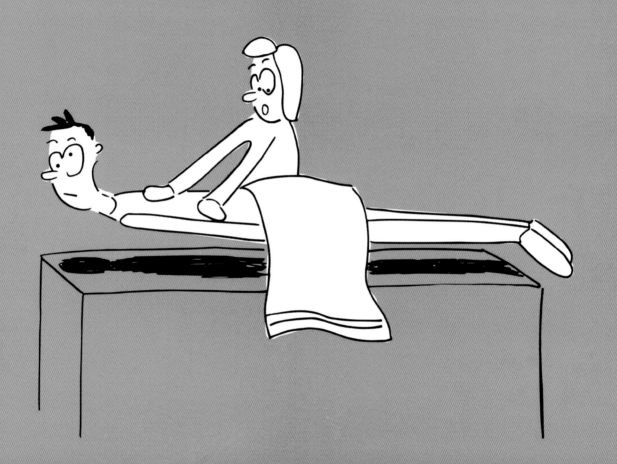

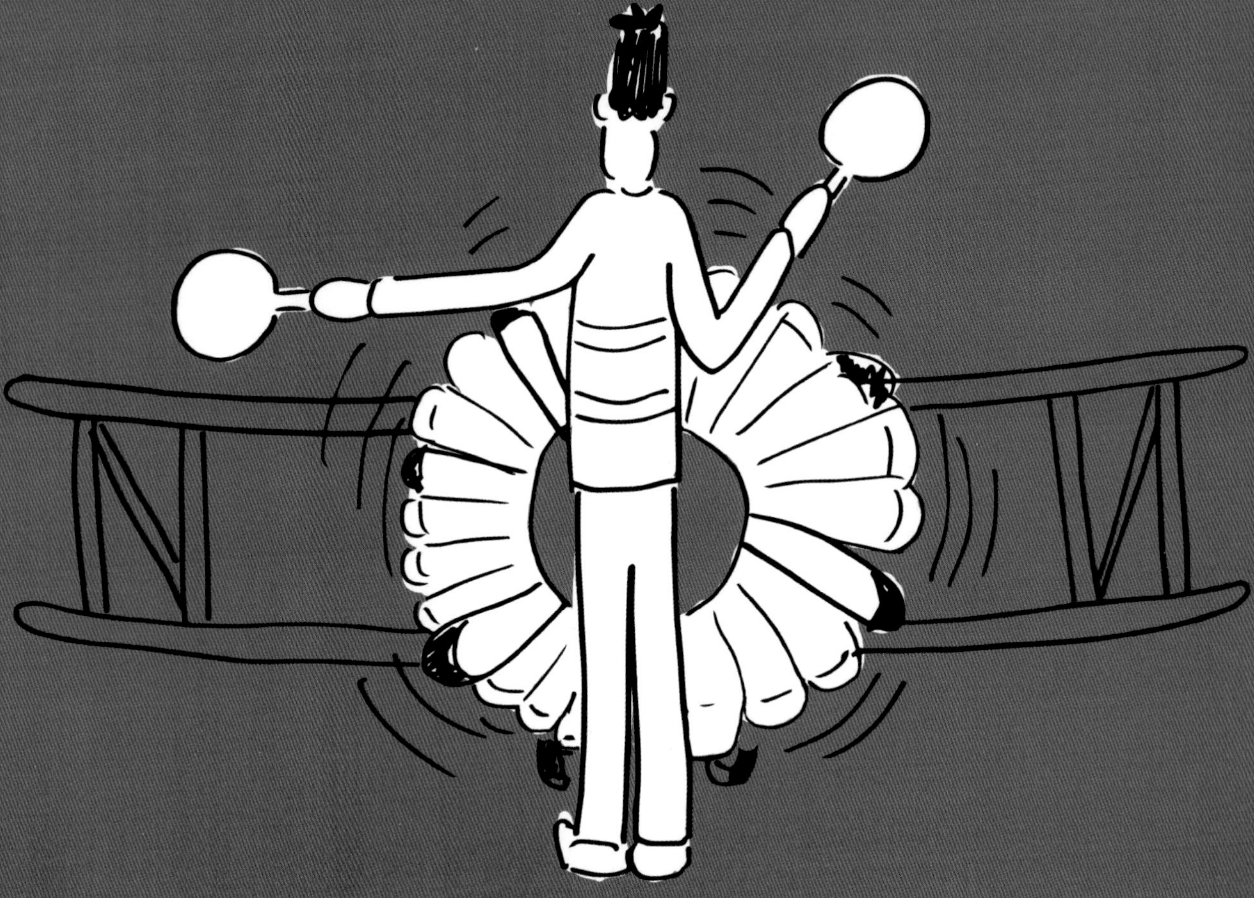

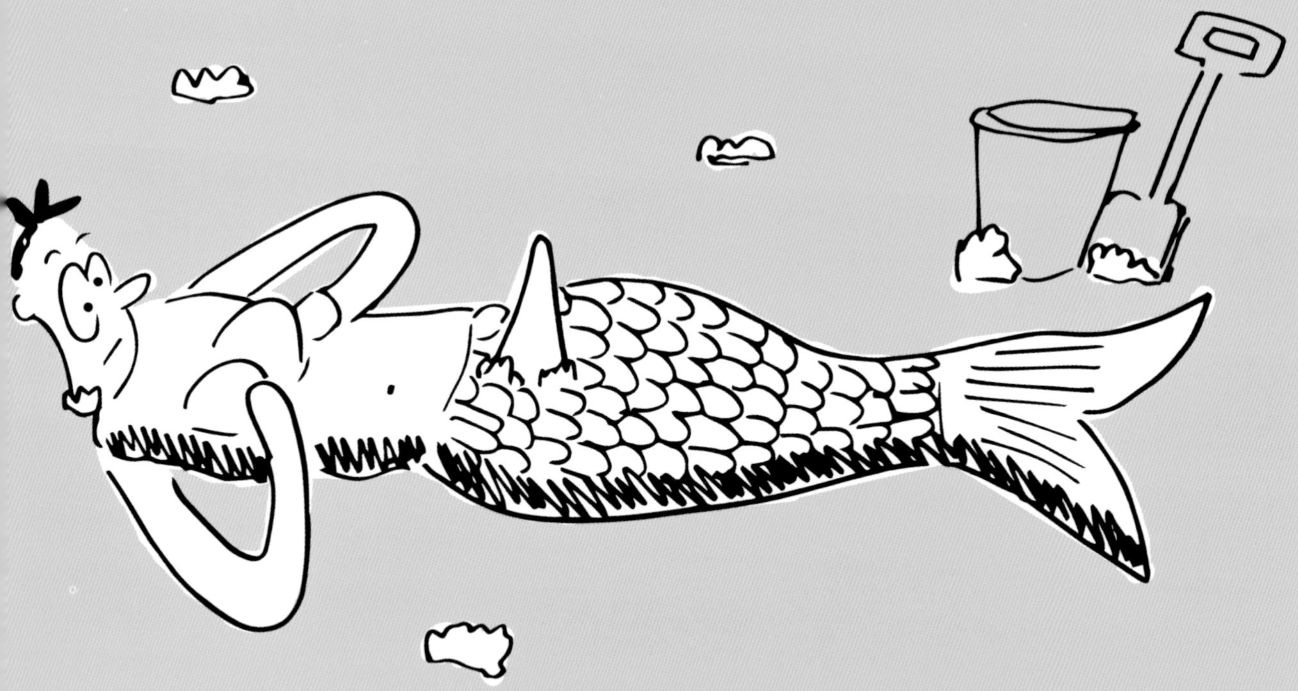

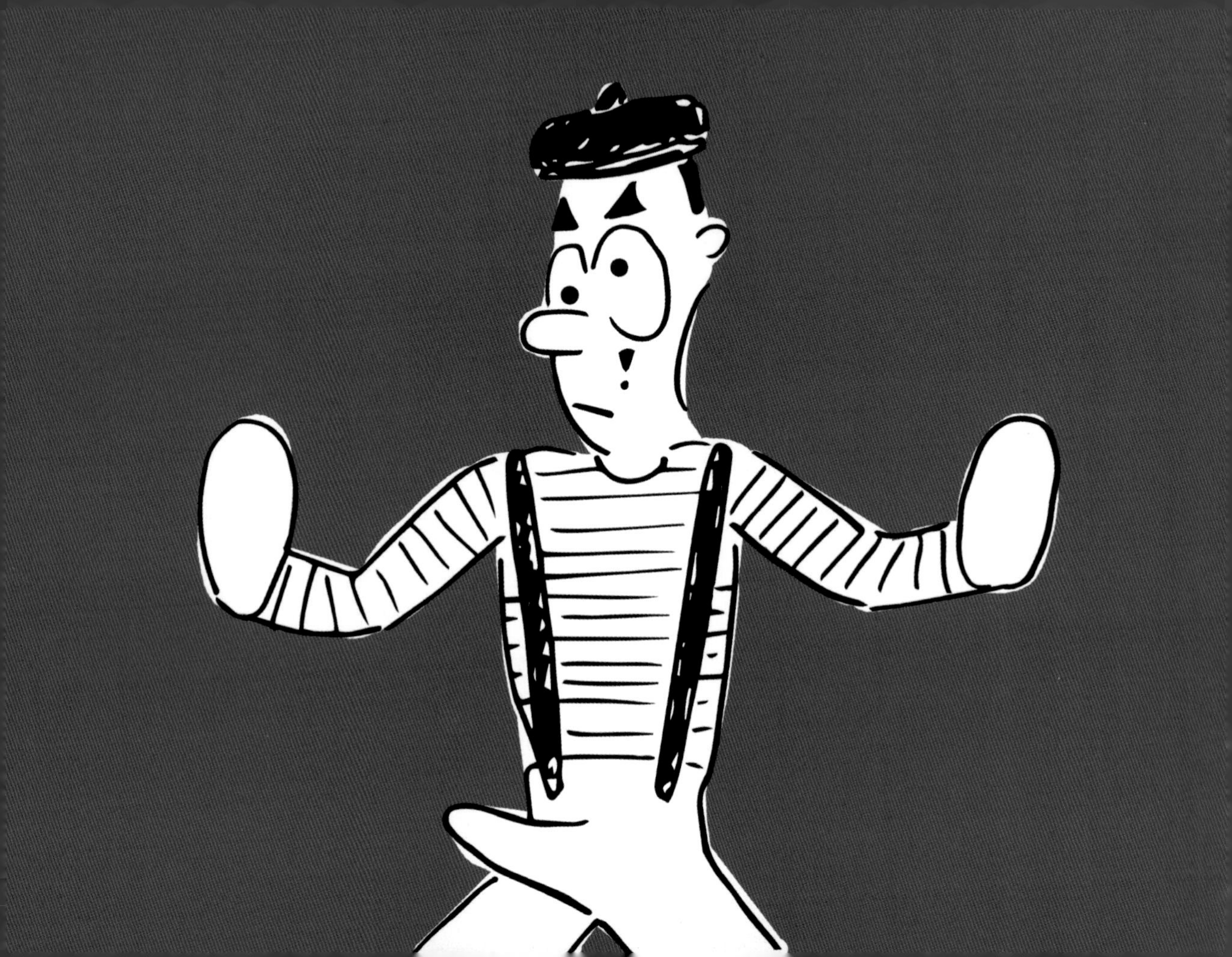

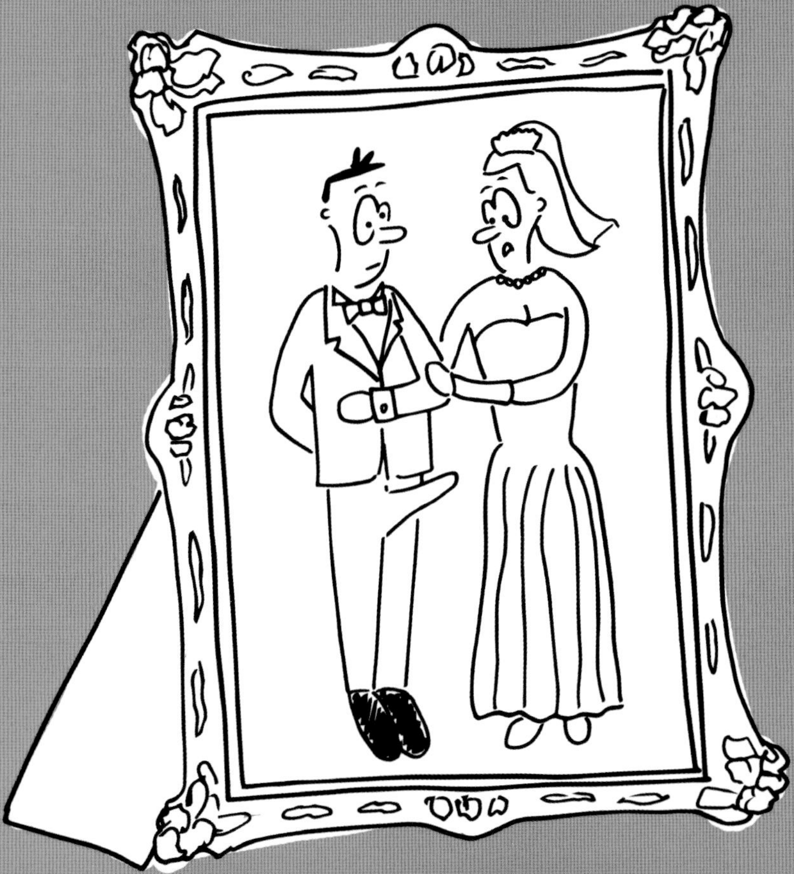

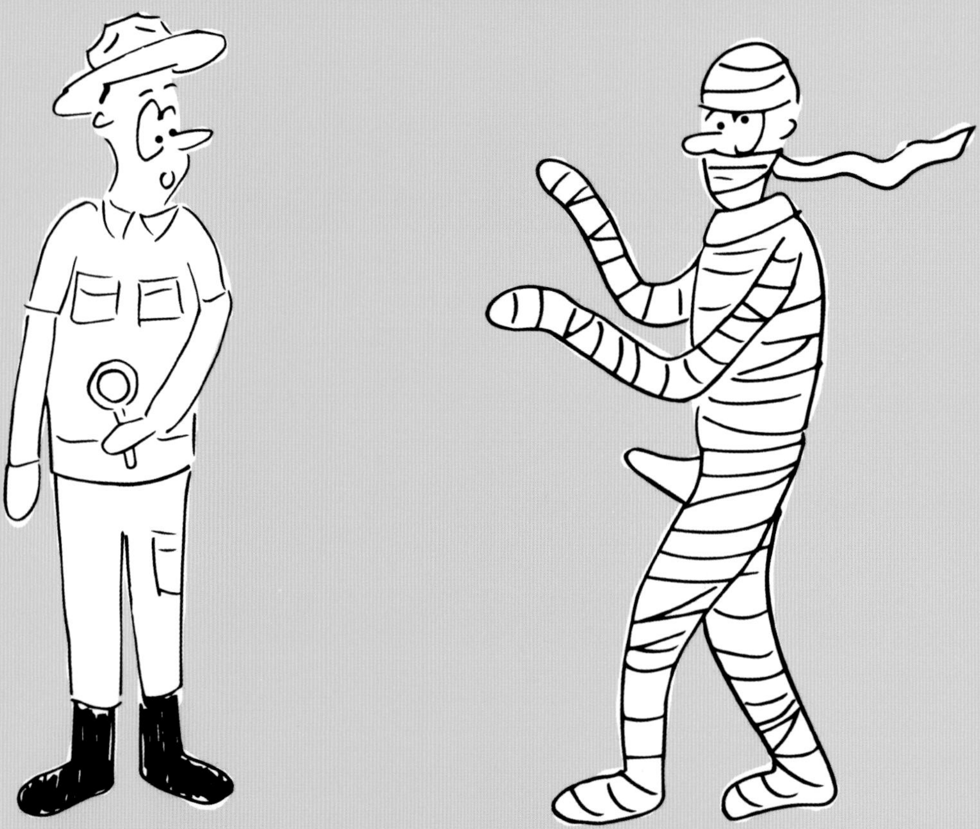

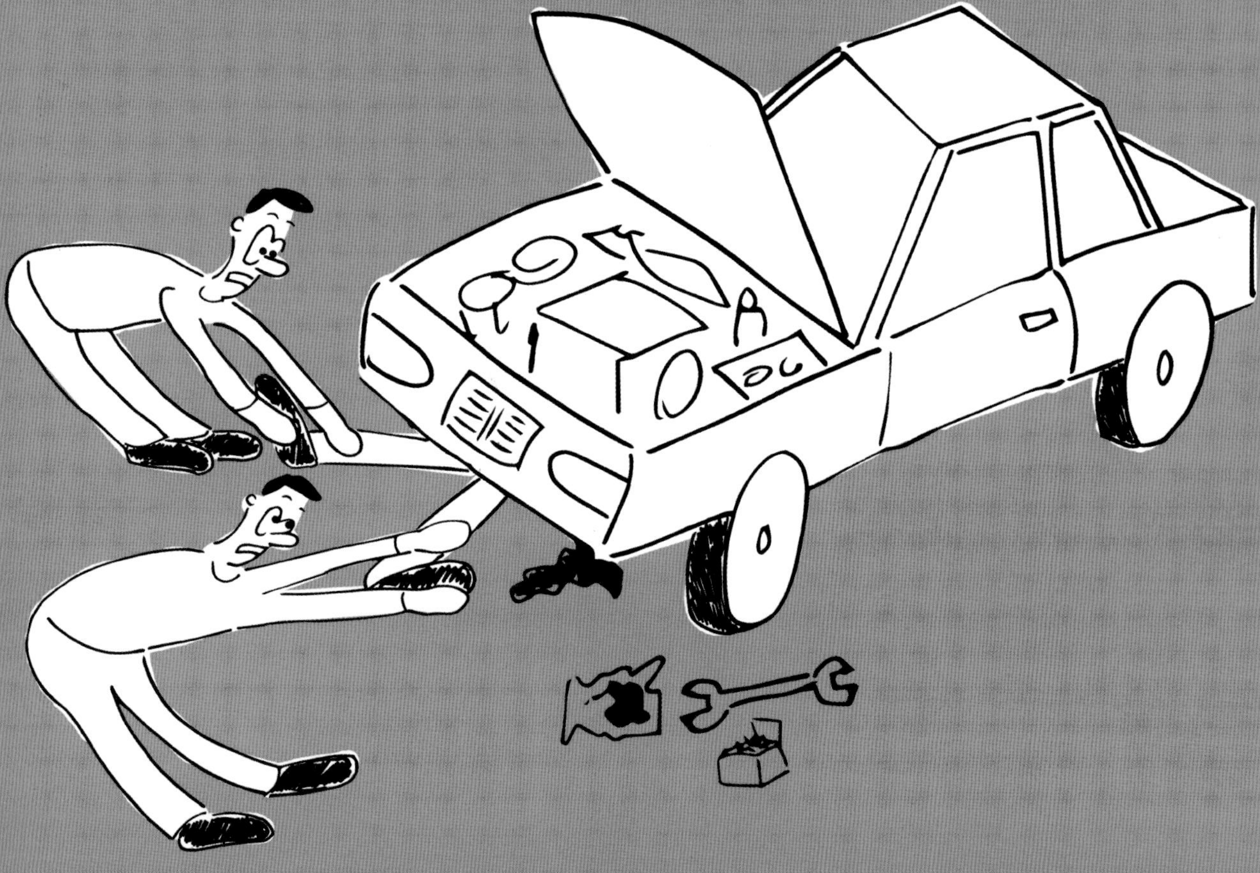

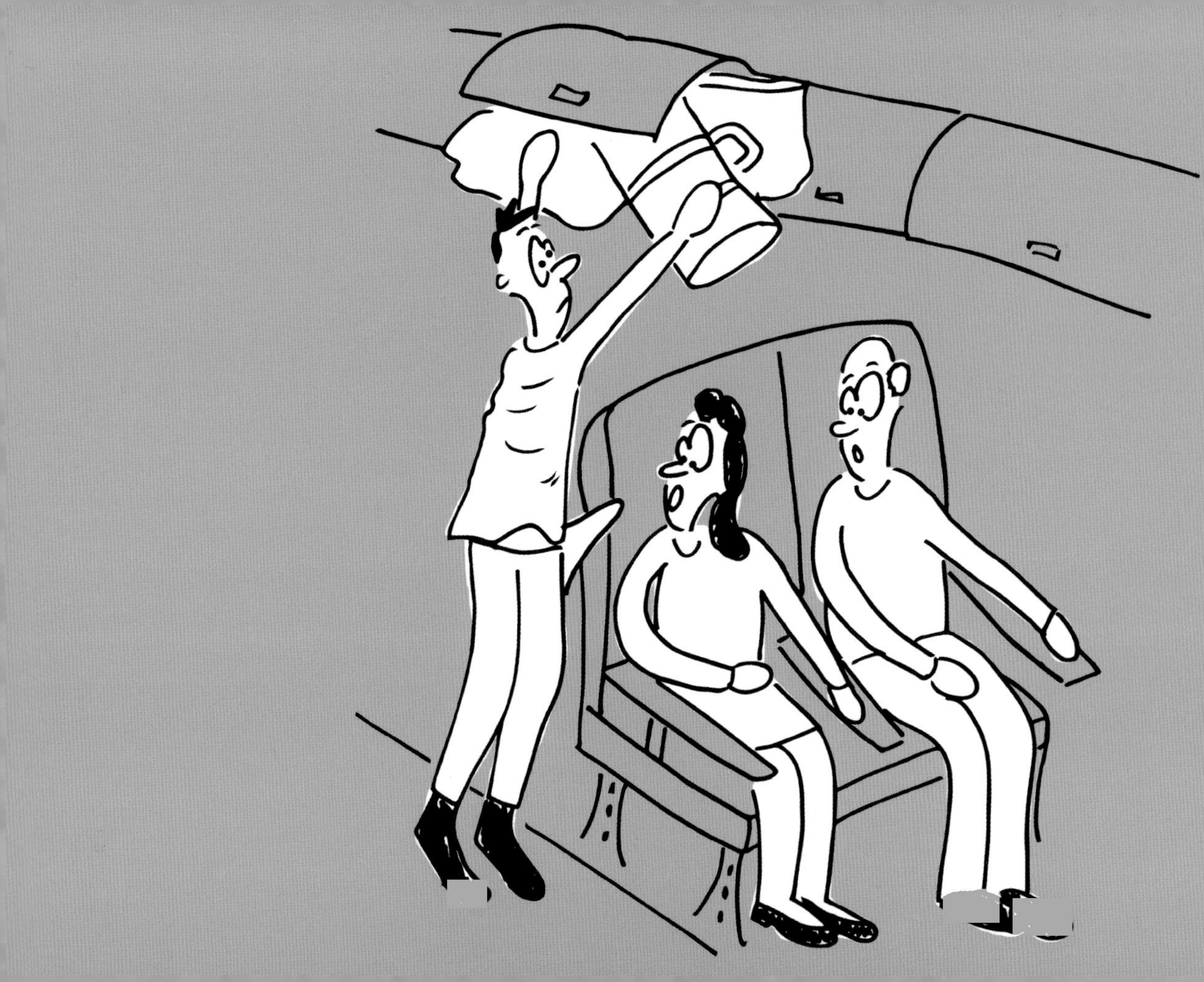

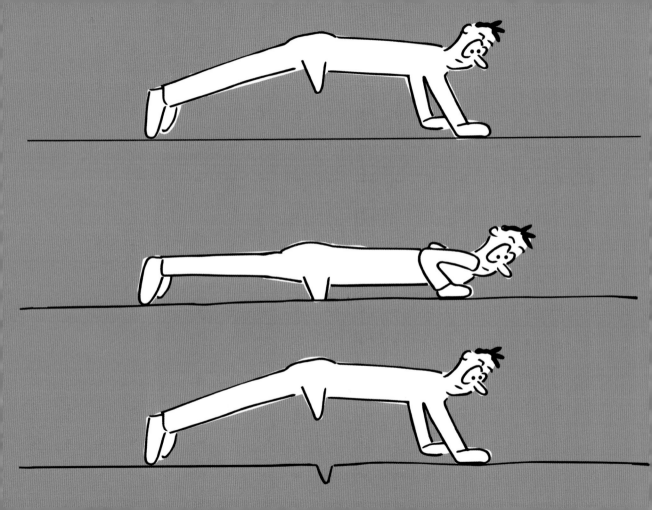

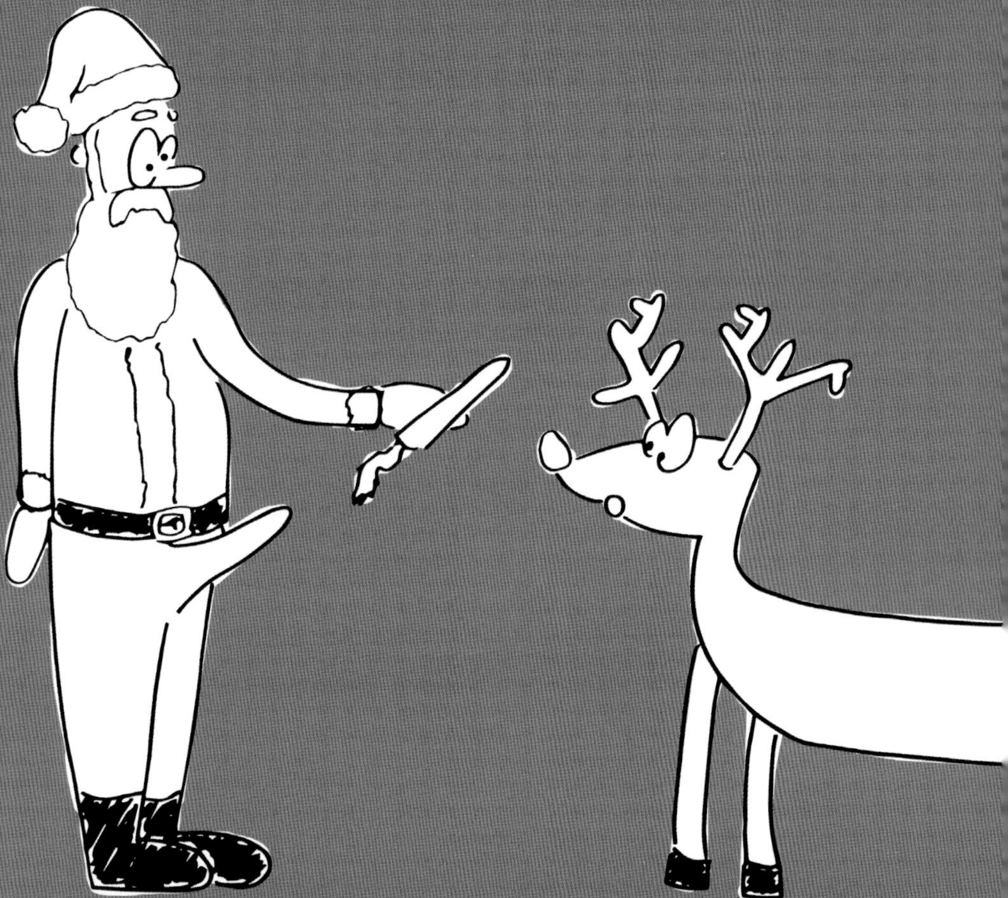

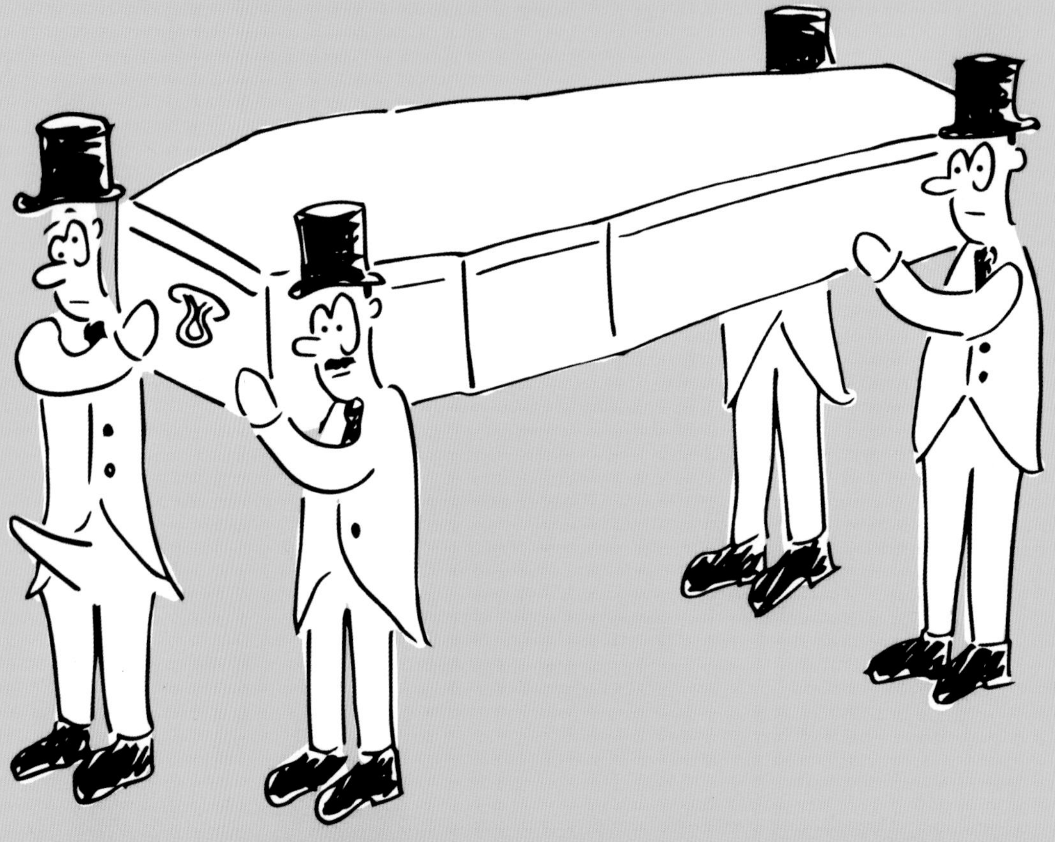

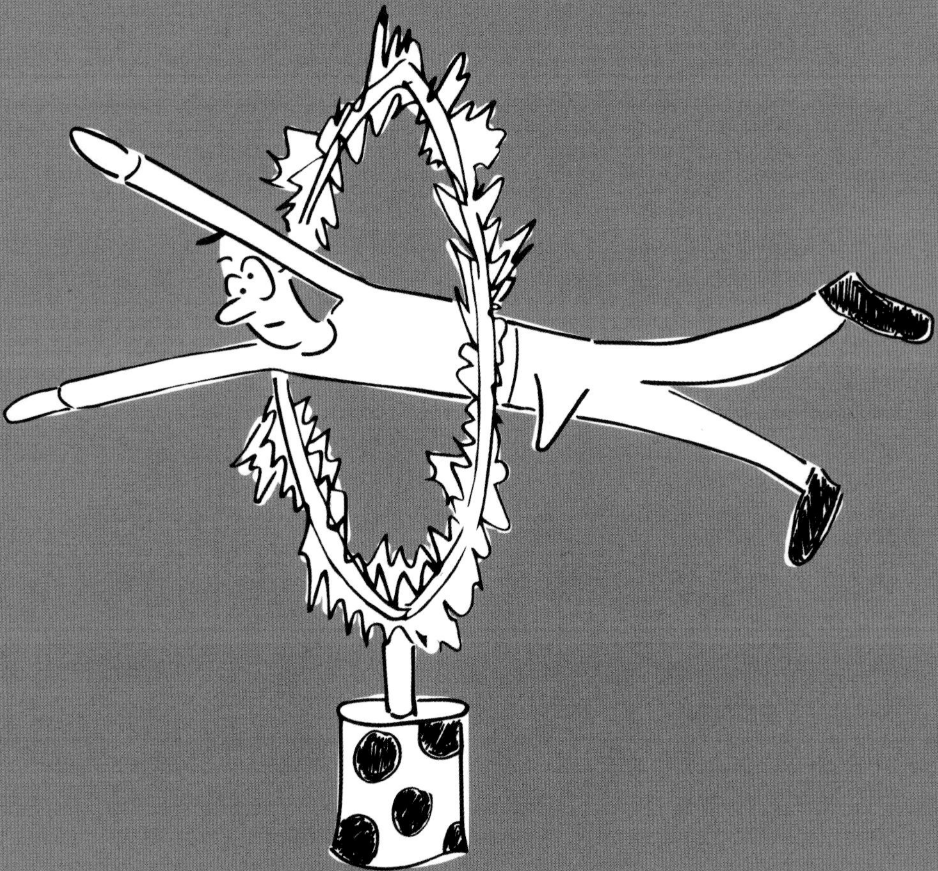

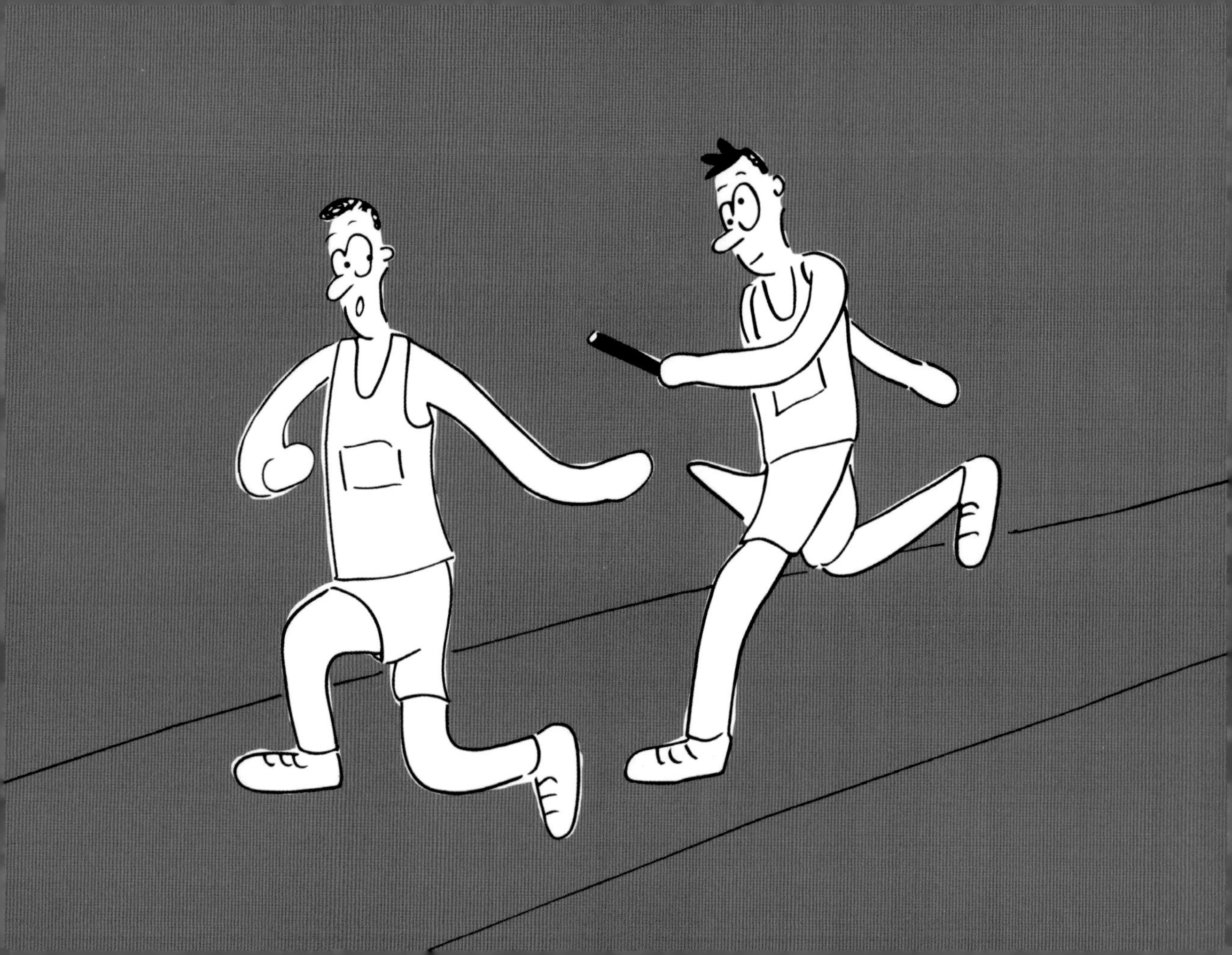

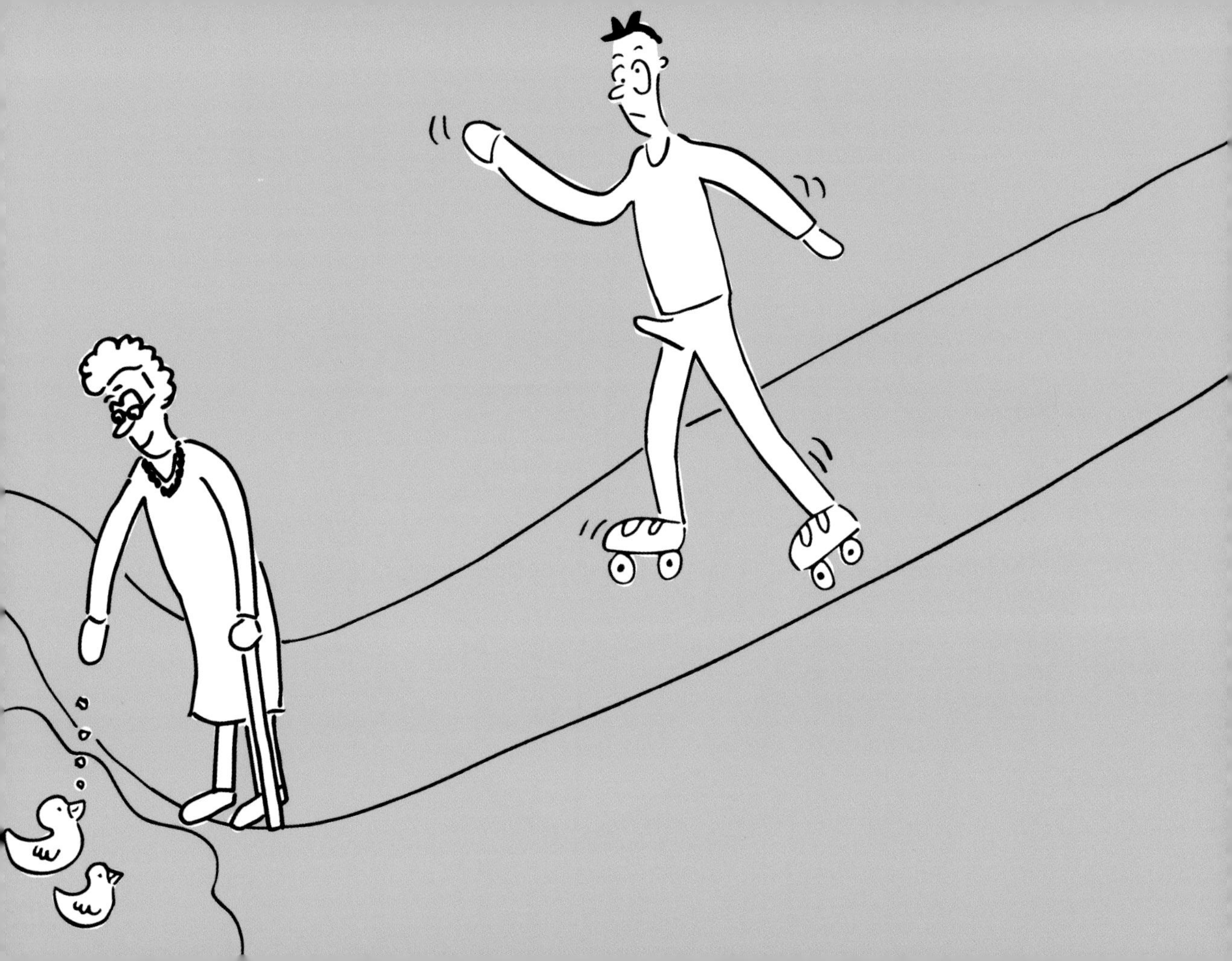

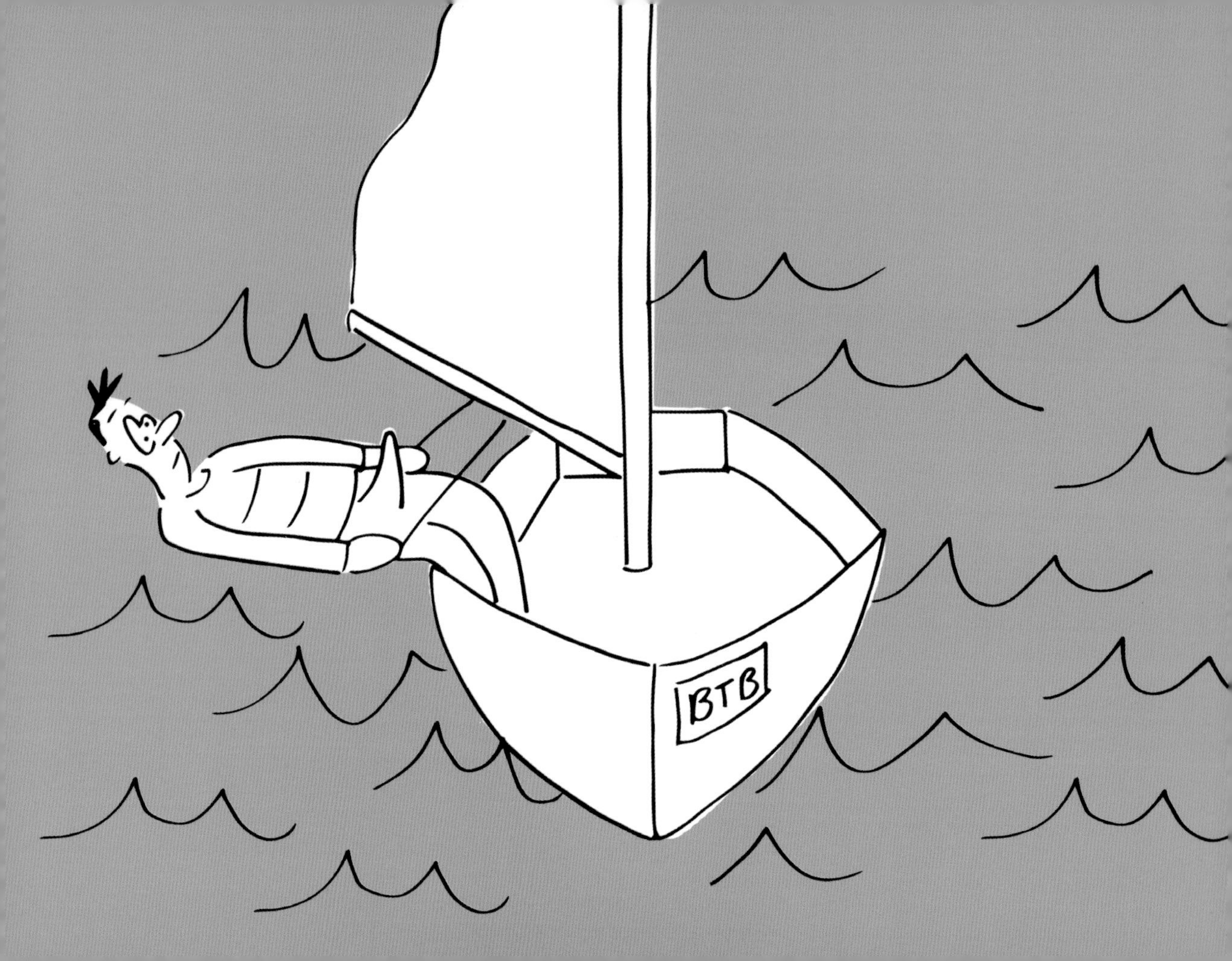
BTB

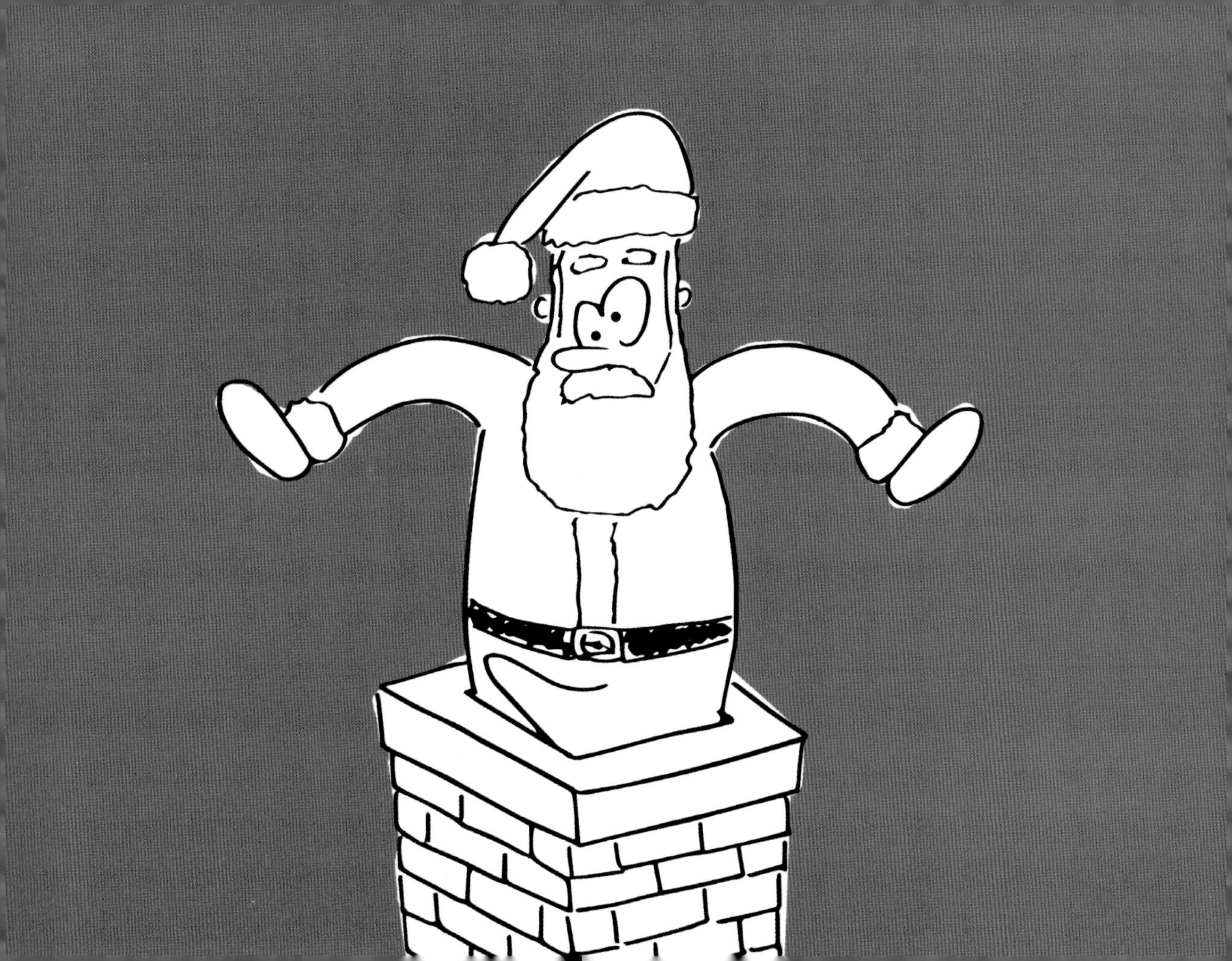

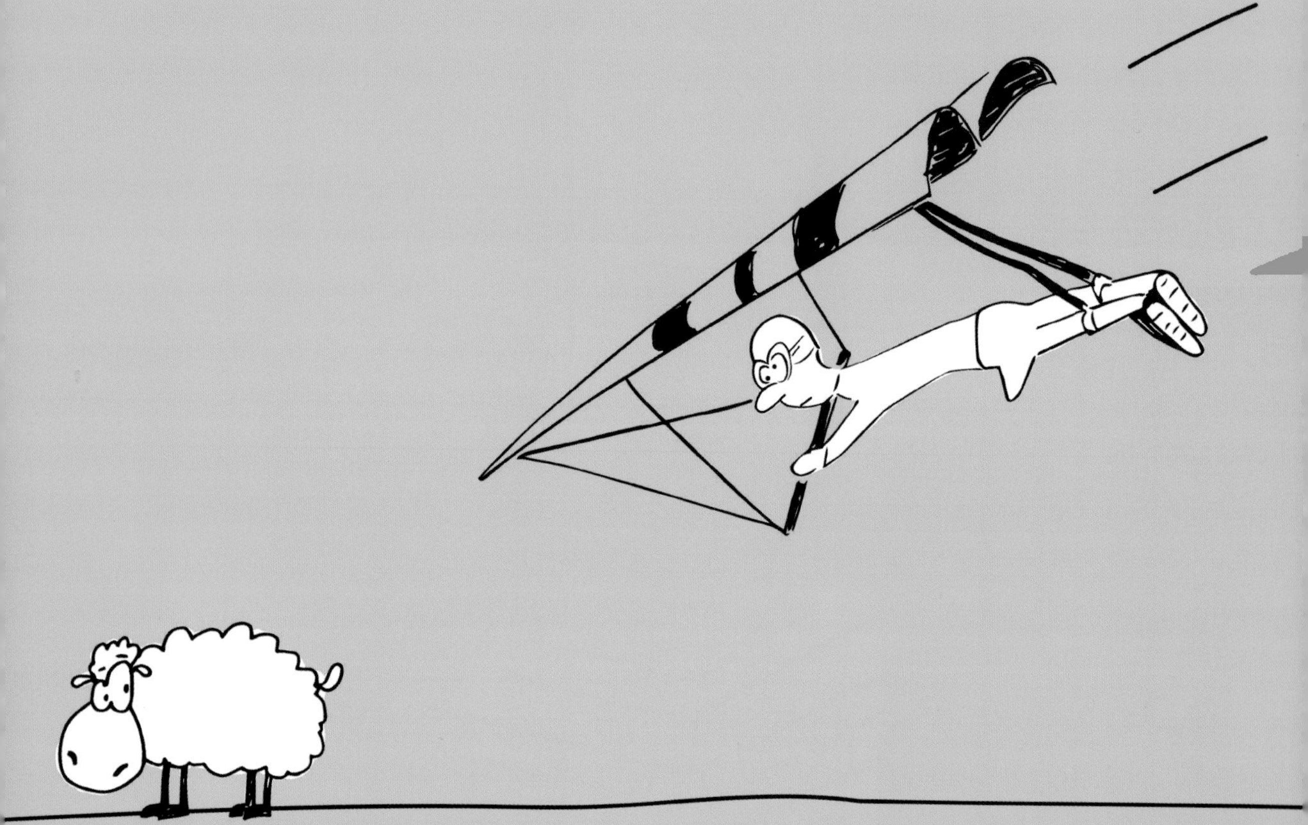

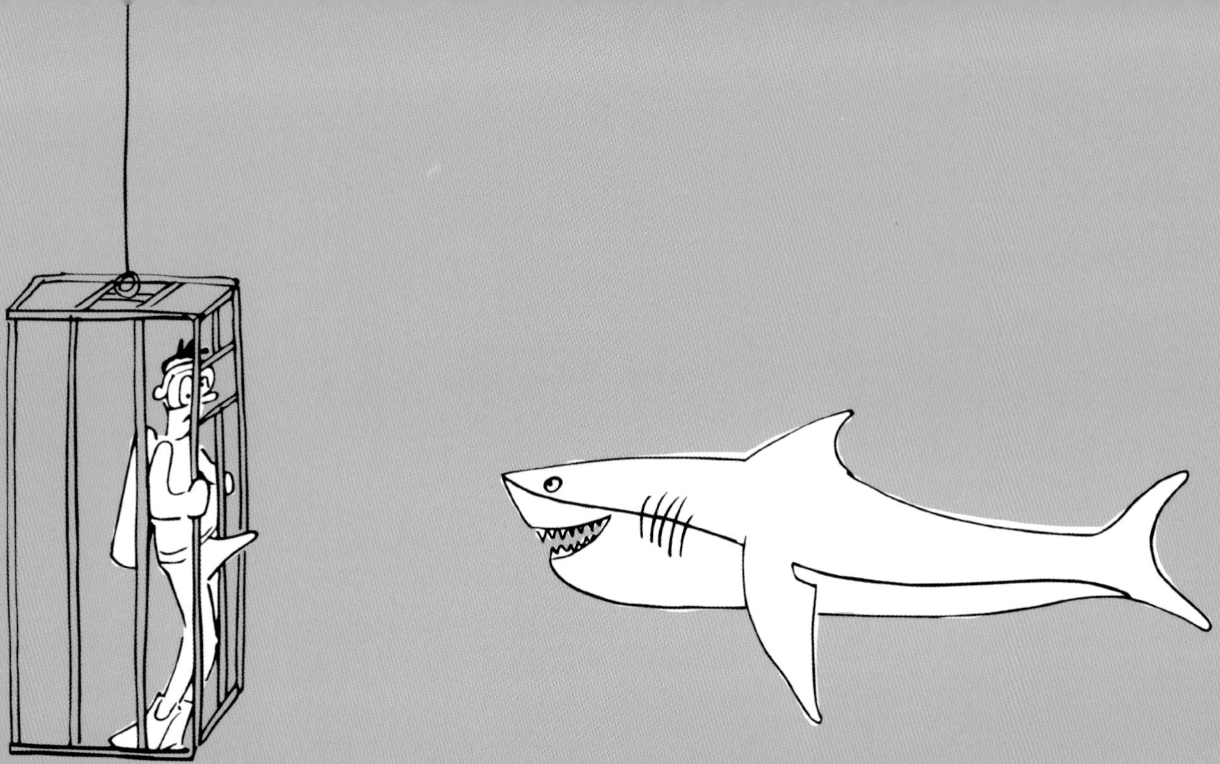

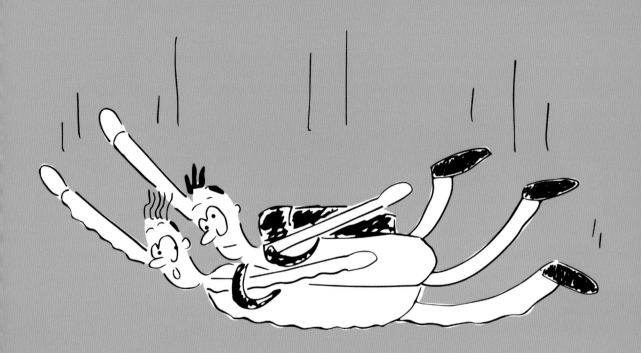

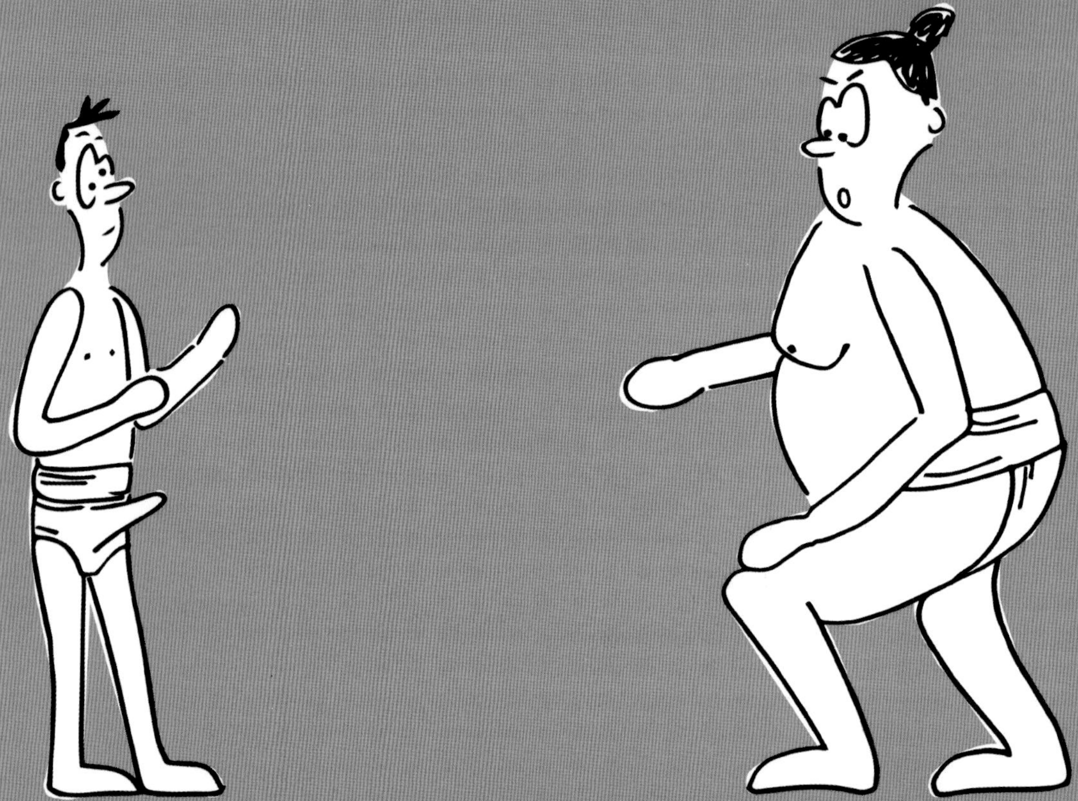

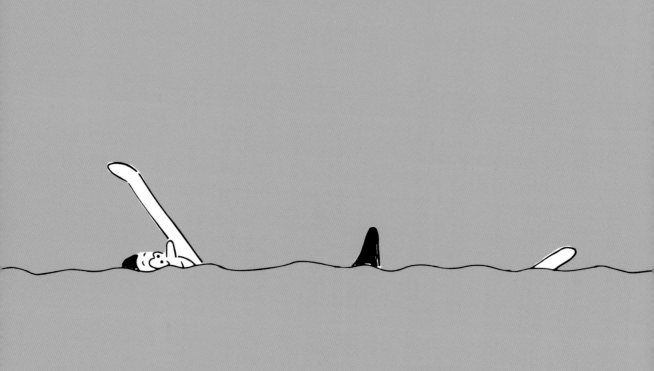

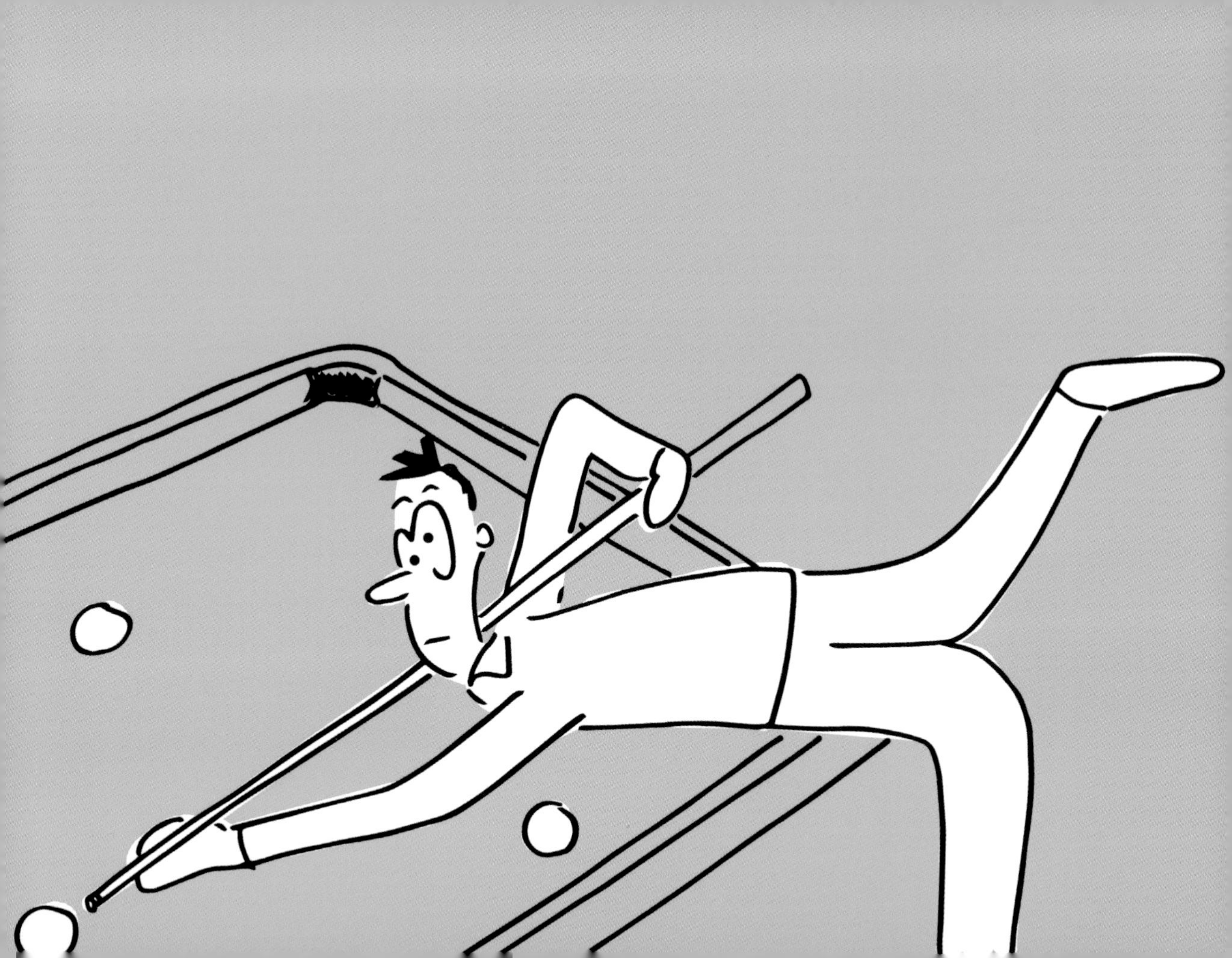

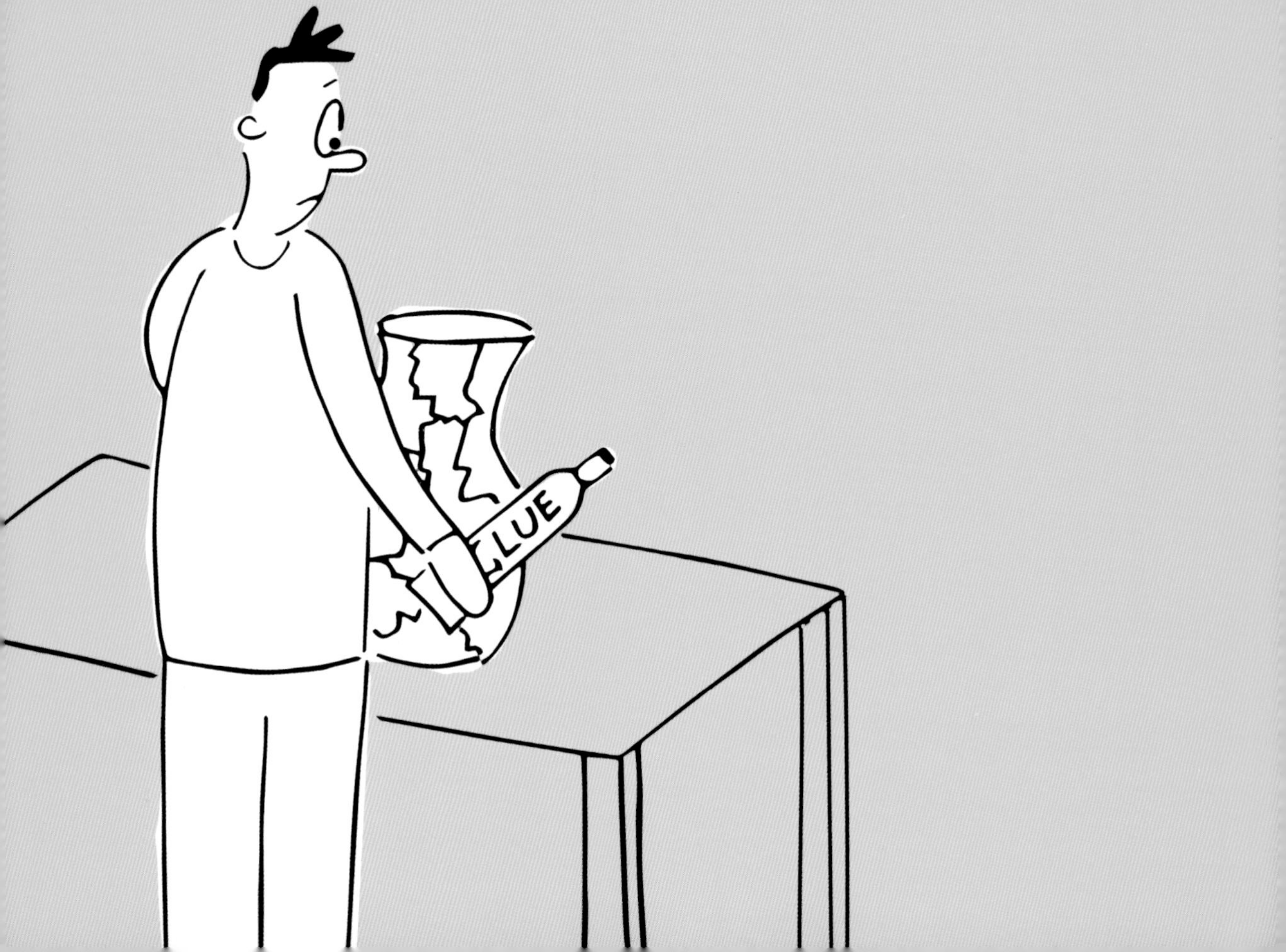
LUE

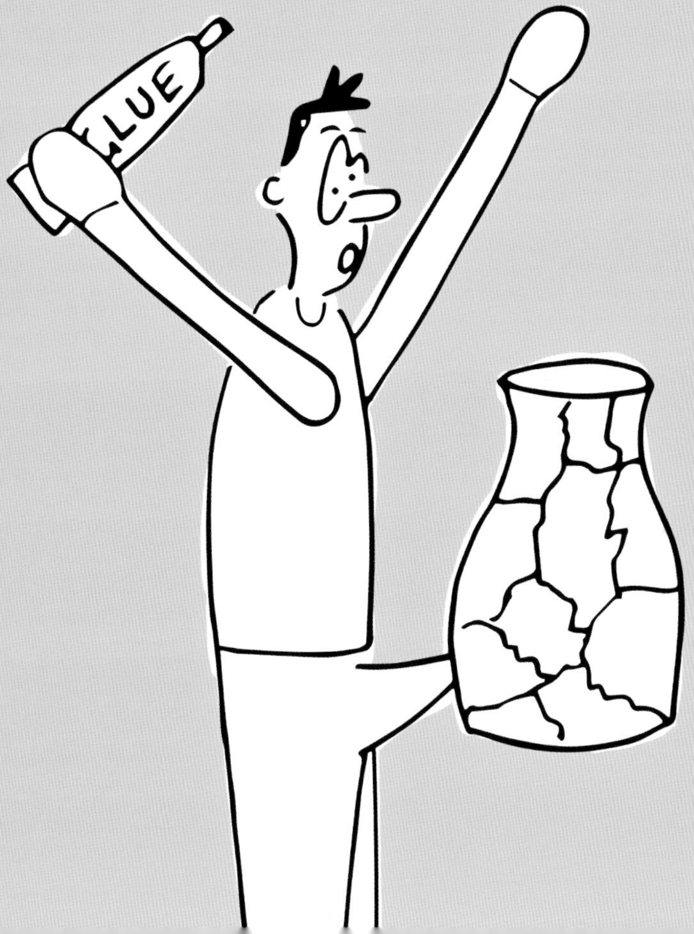
LUE

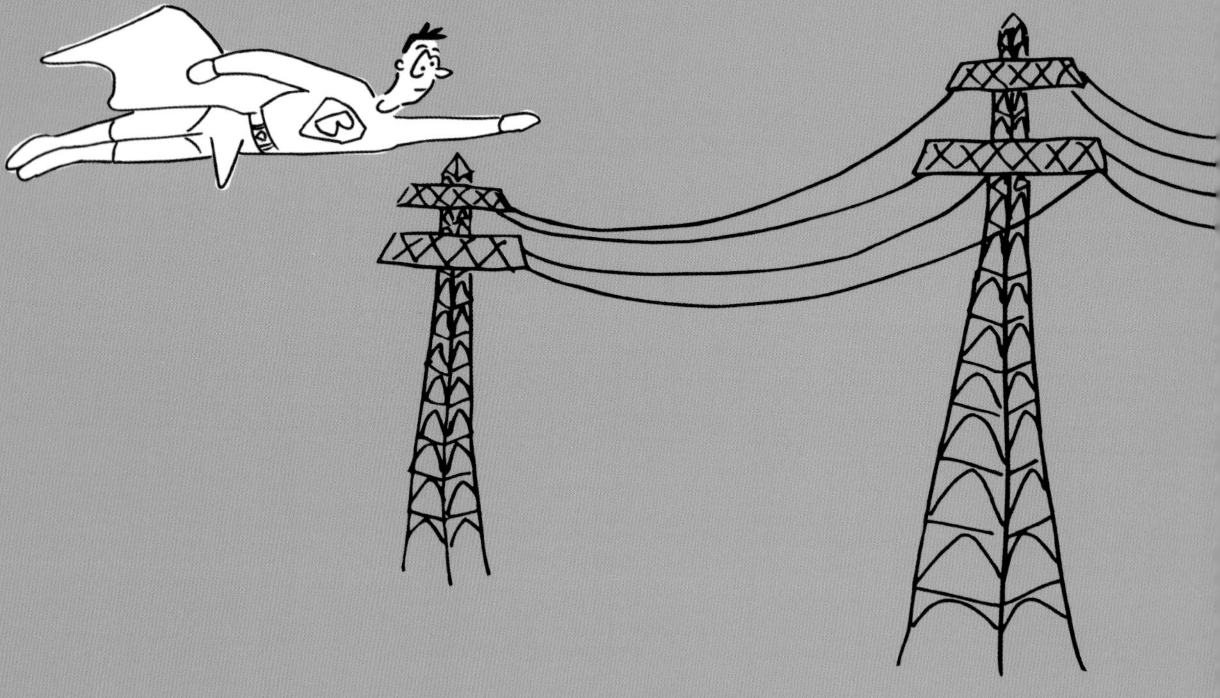

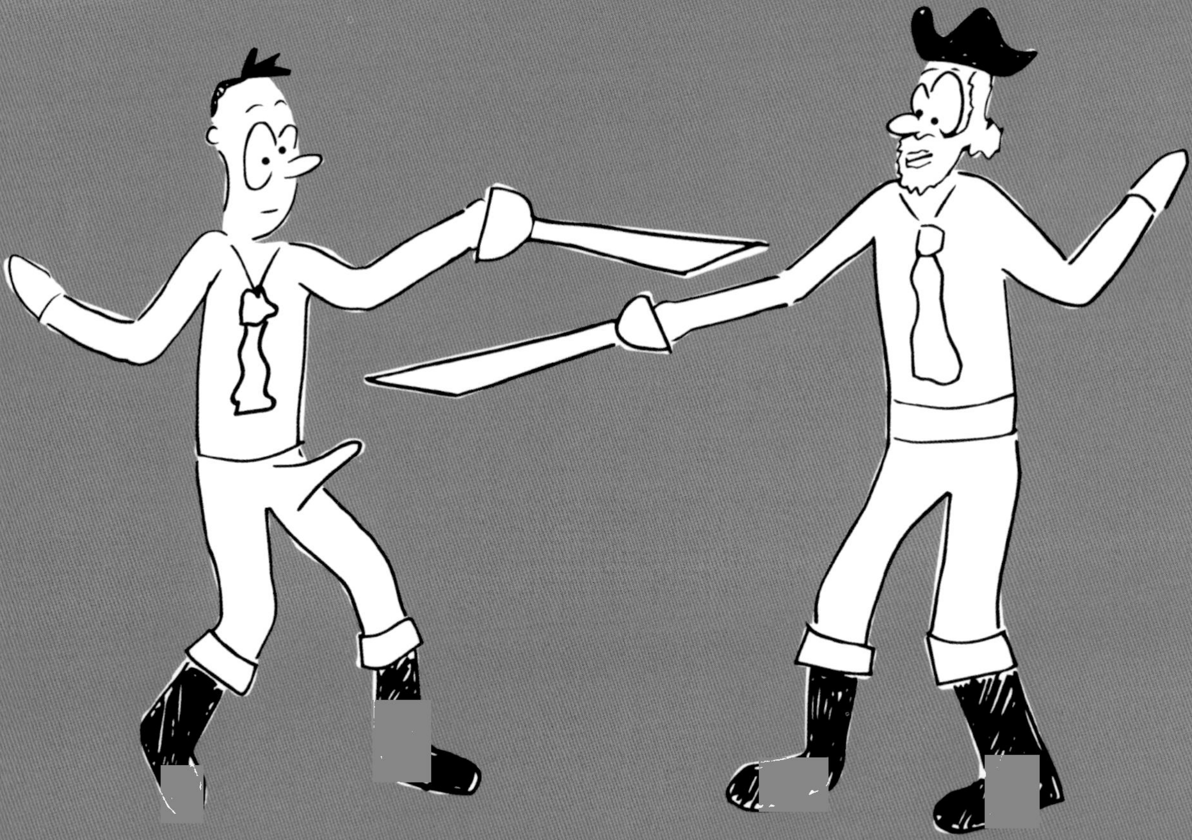

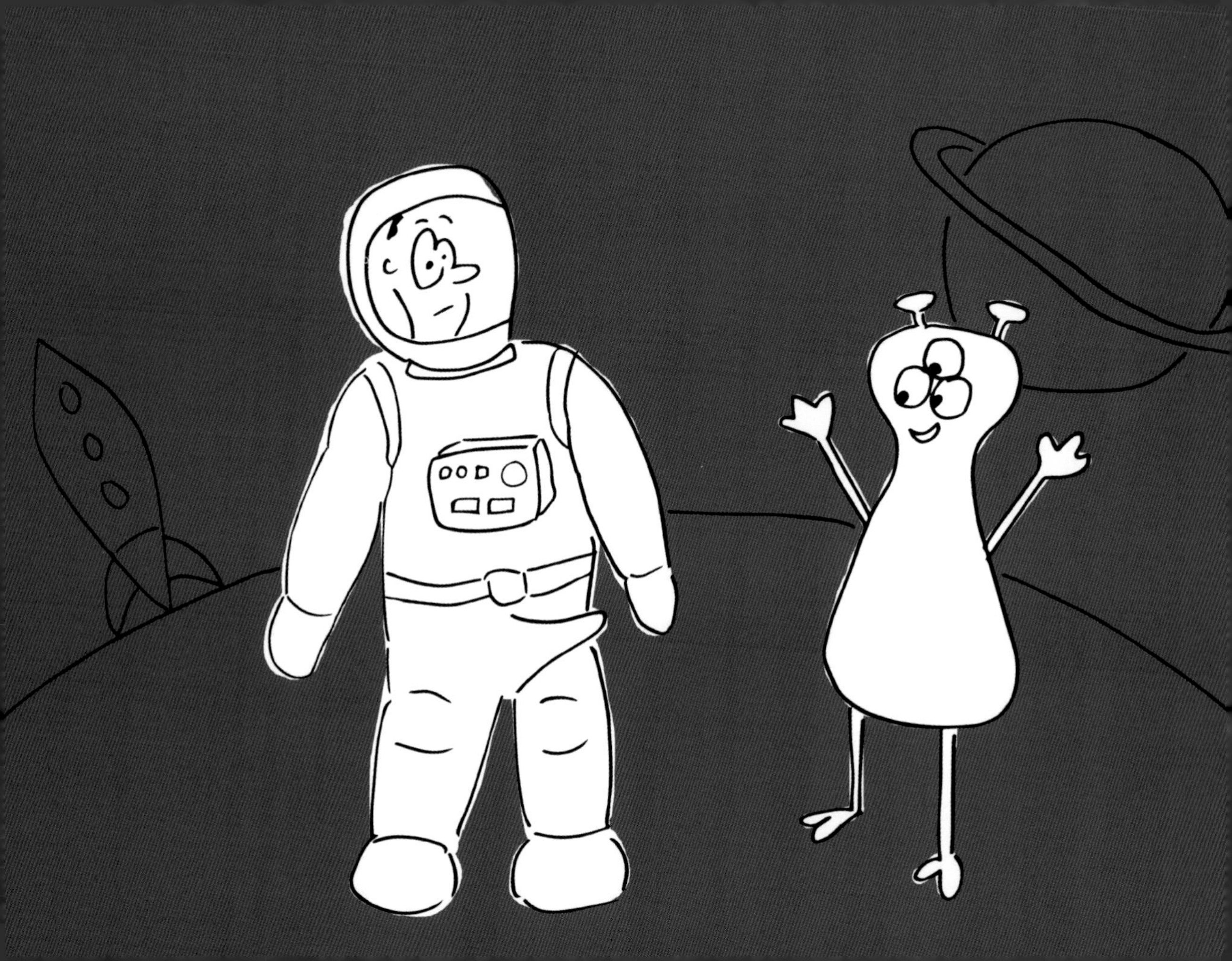

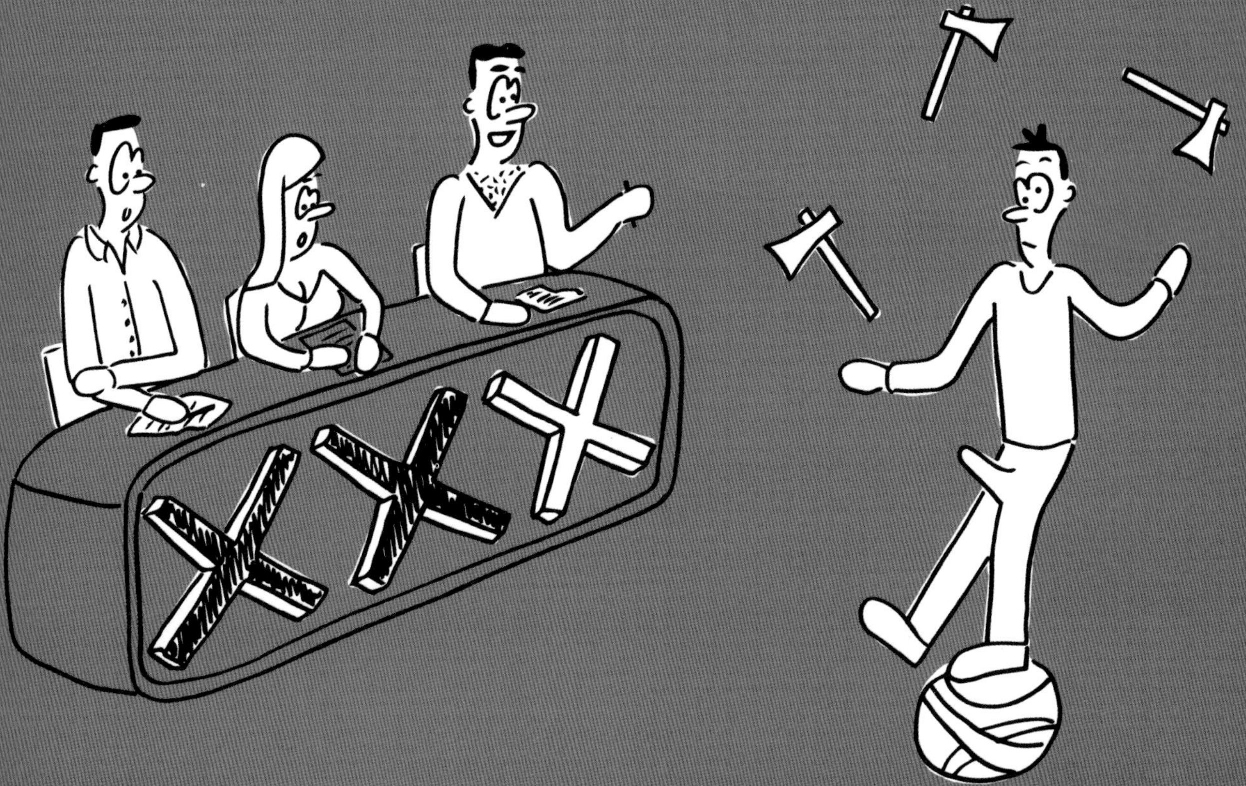

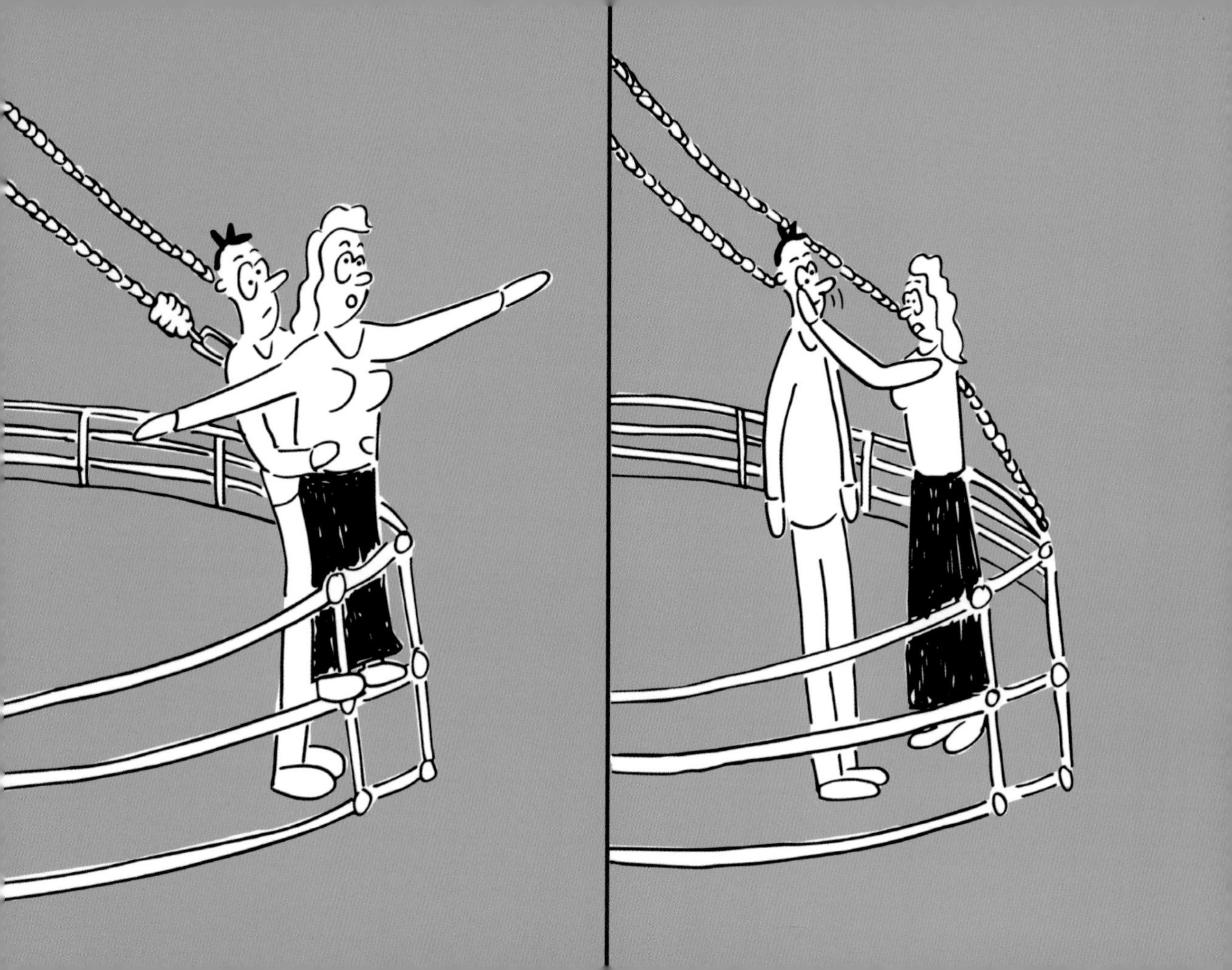

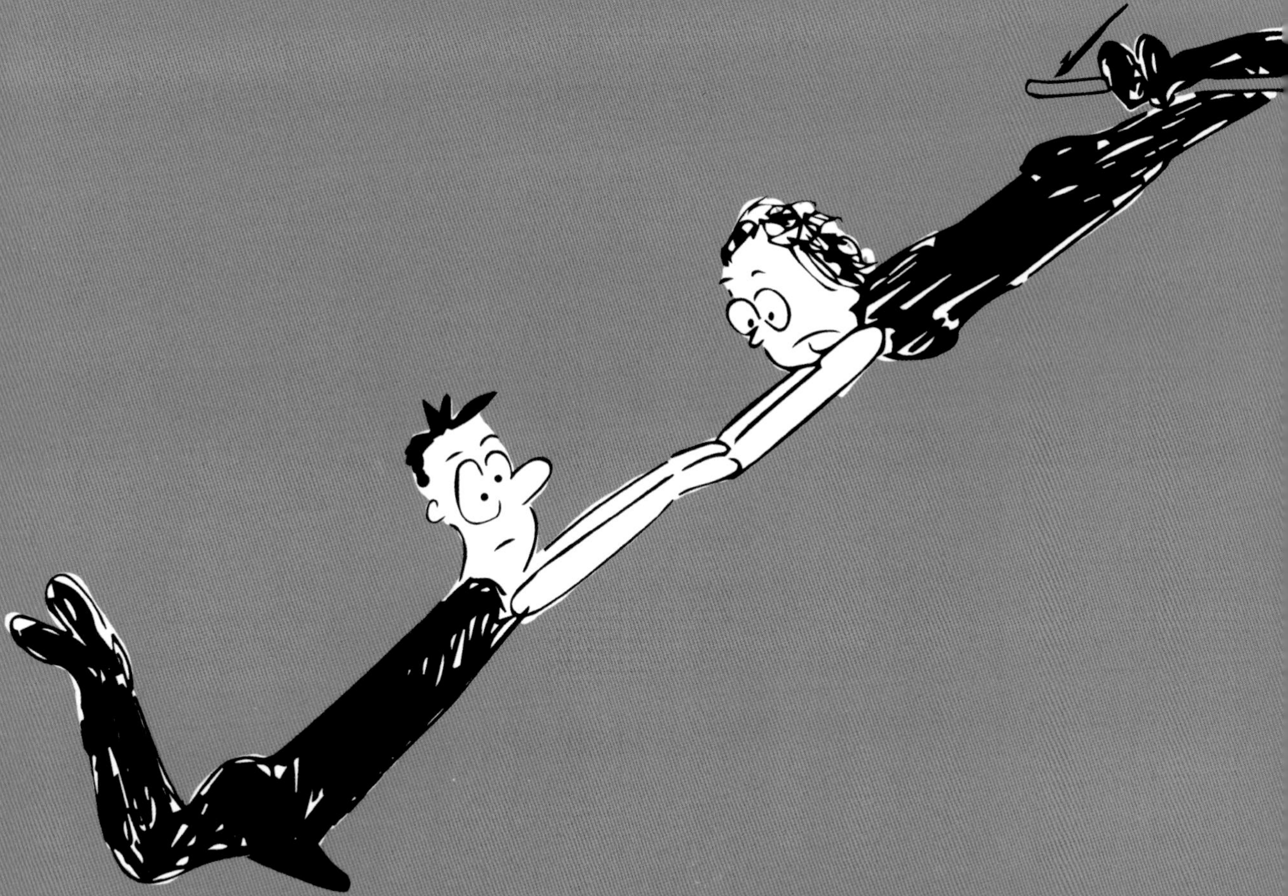

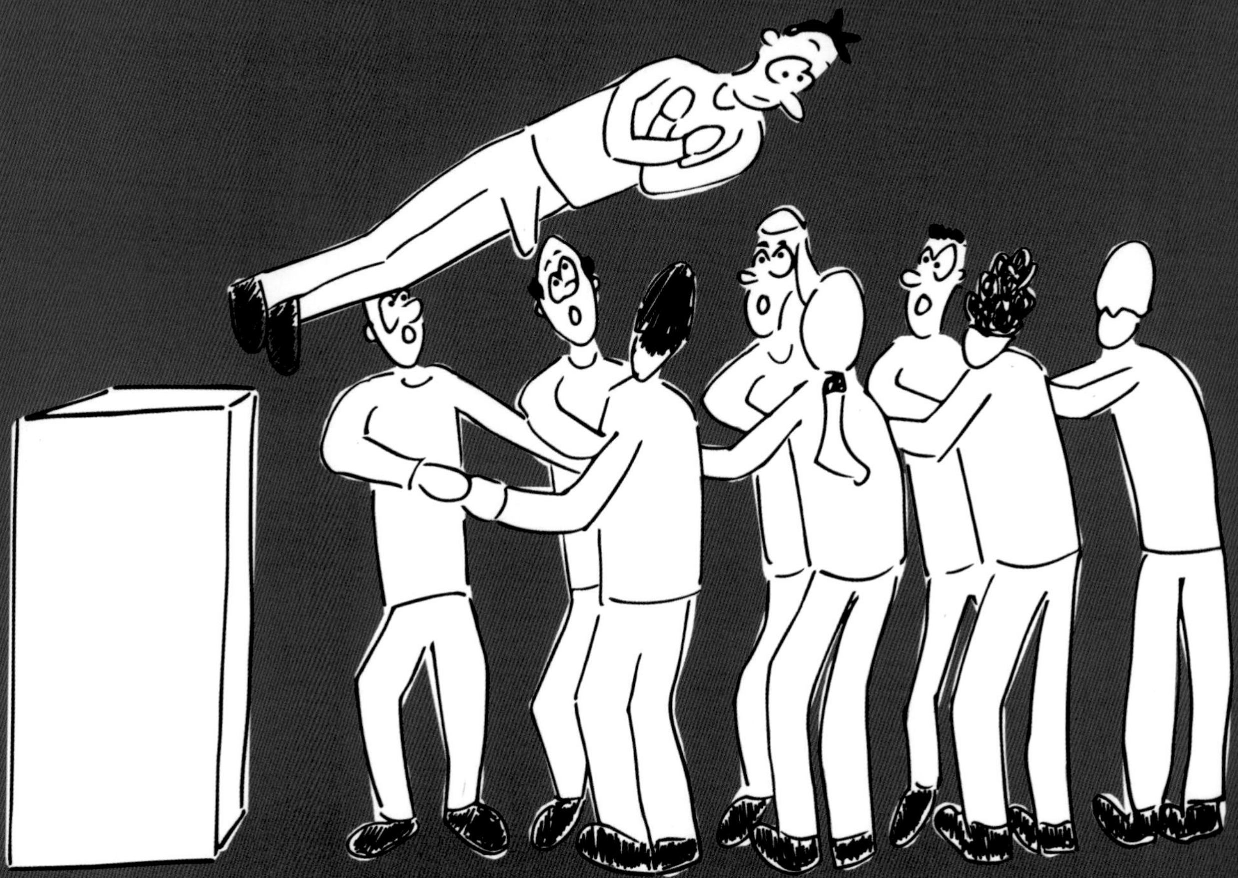

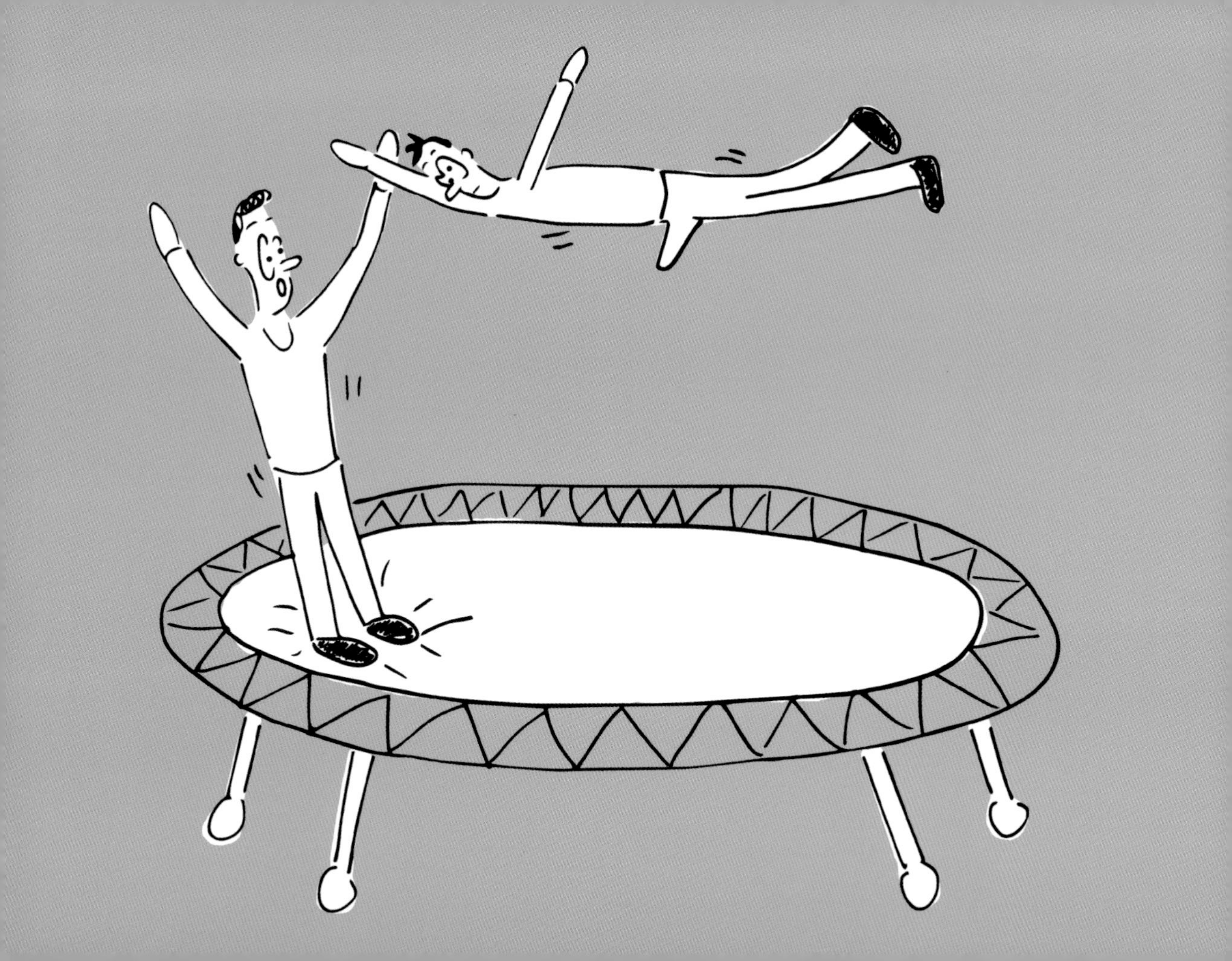

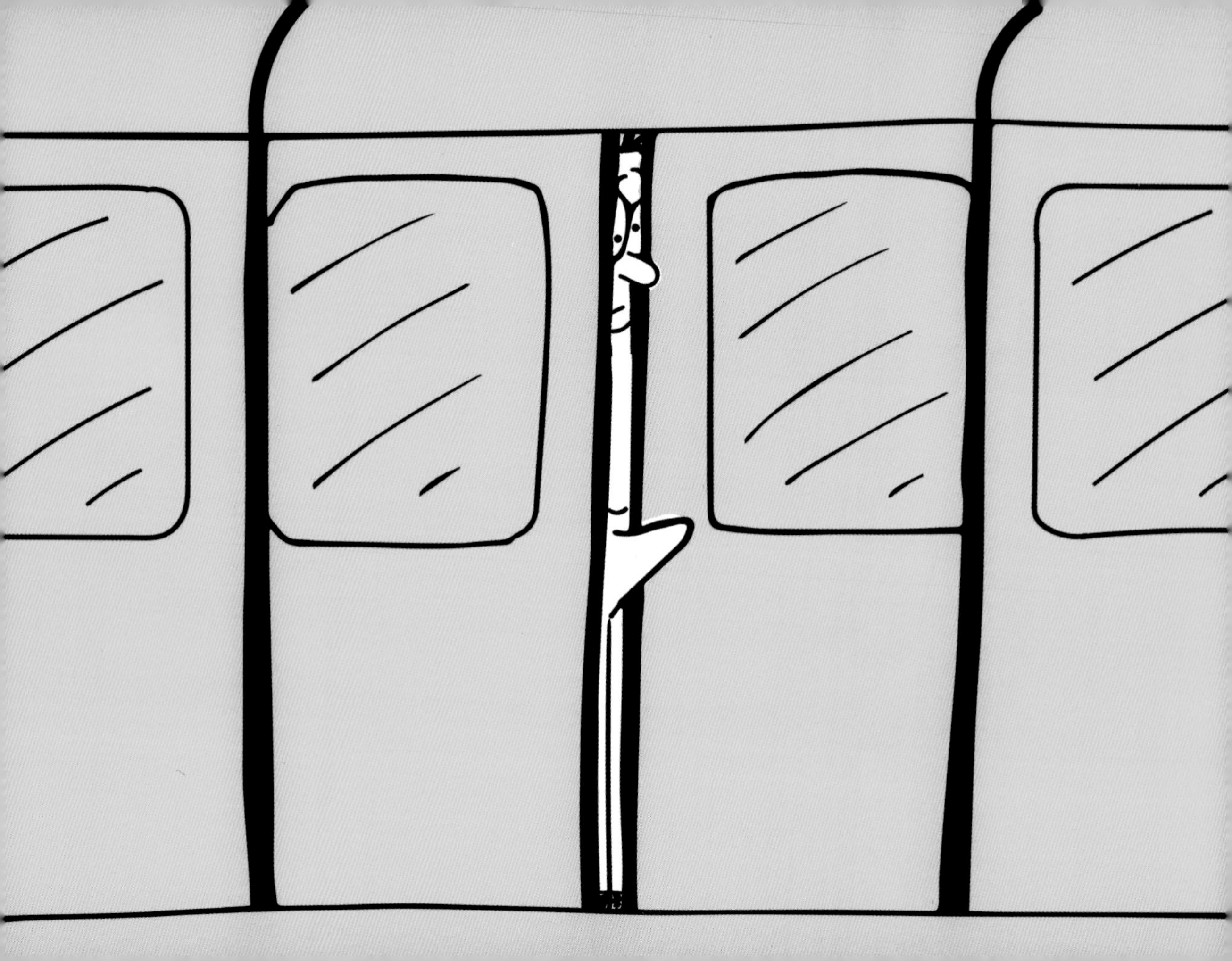

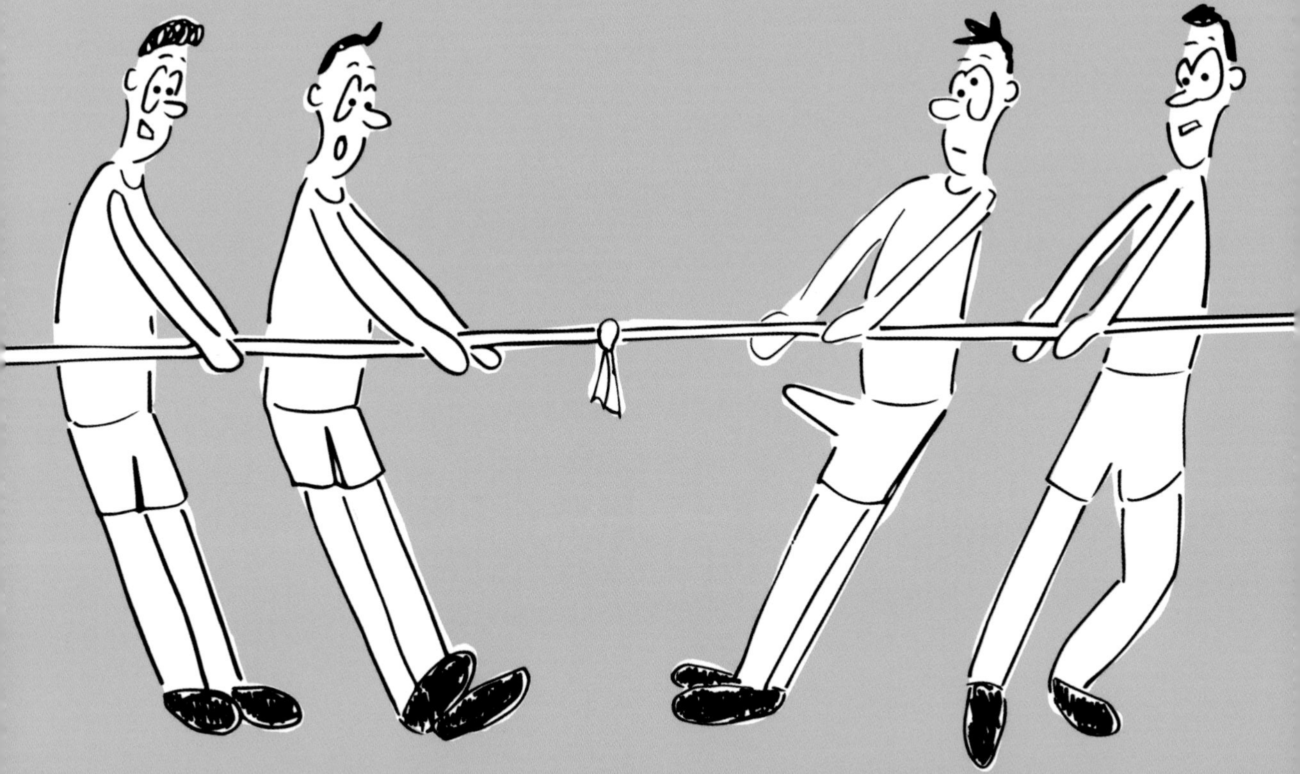

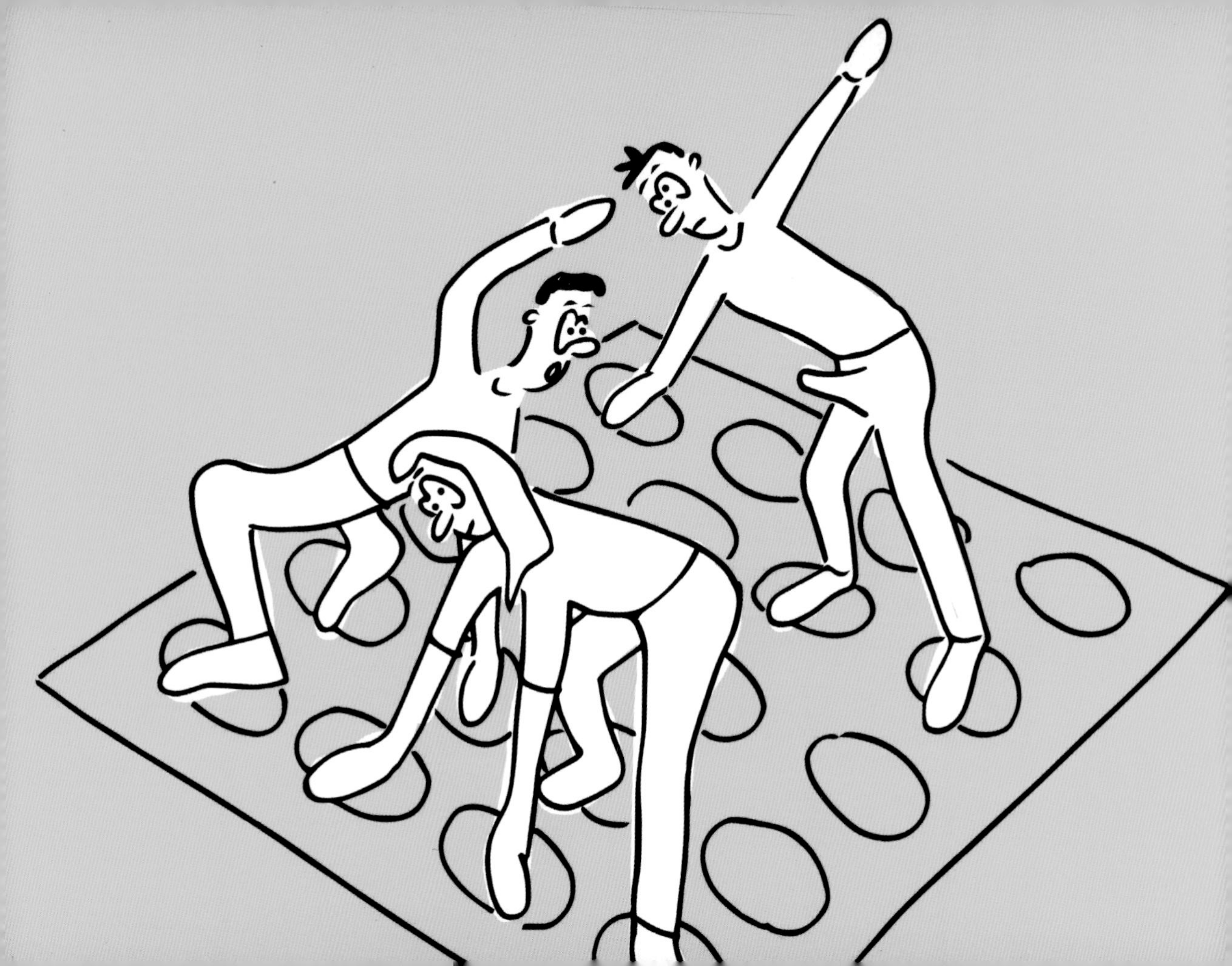

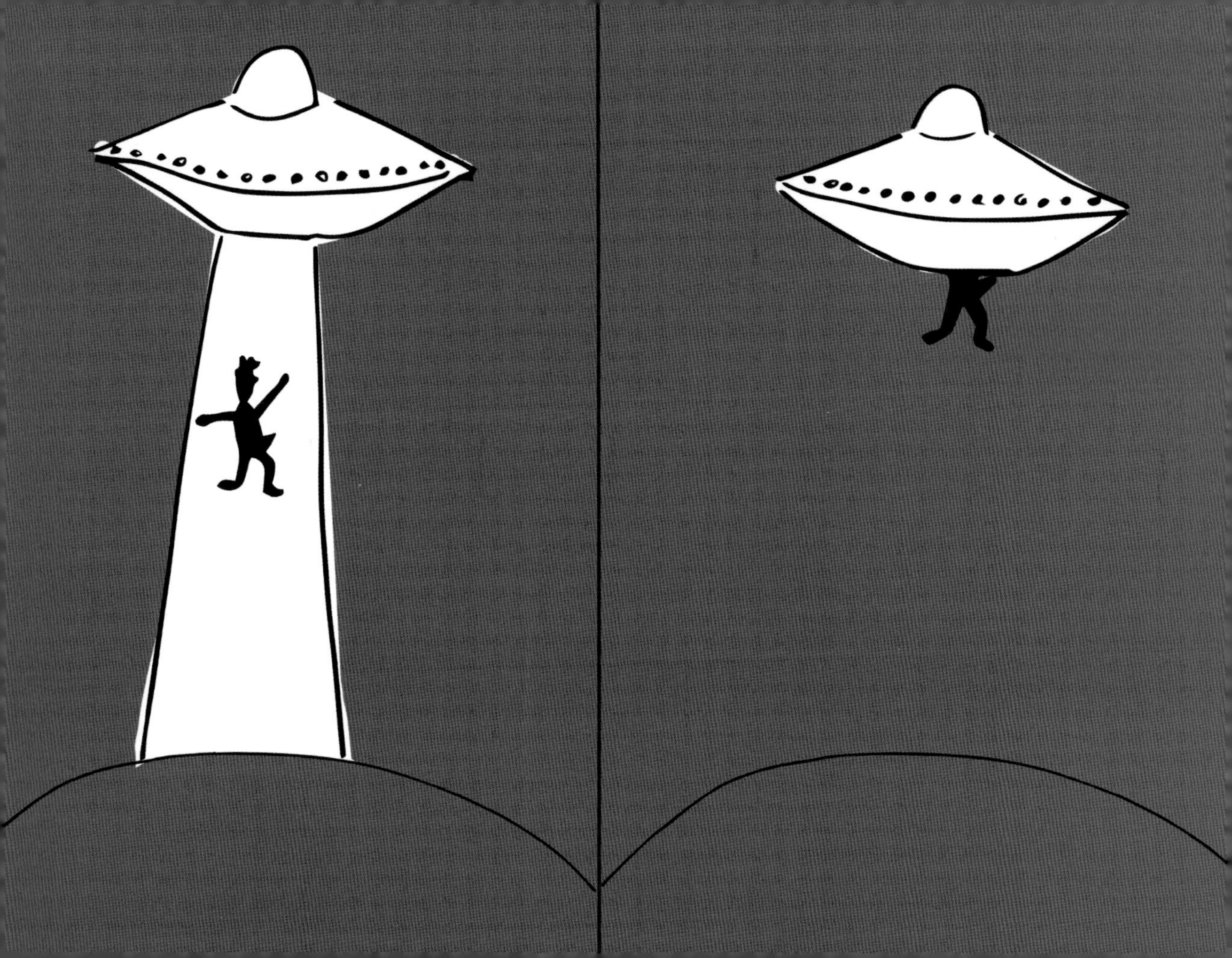

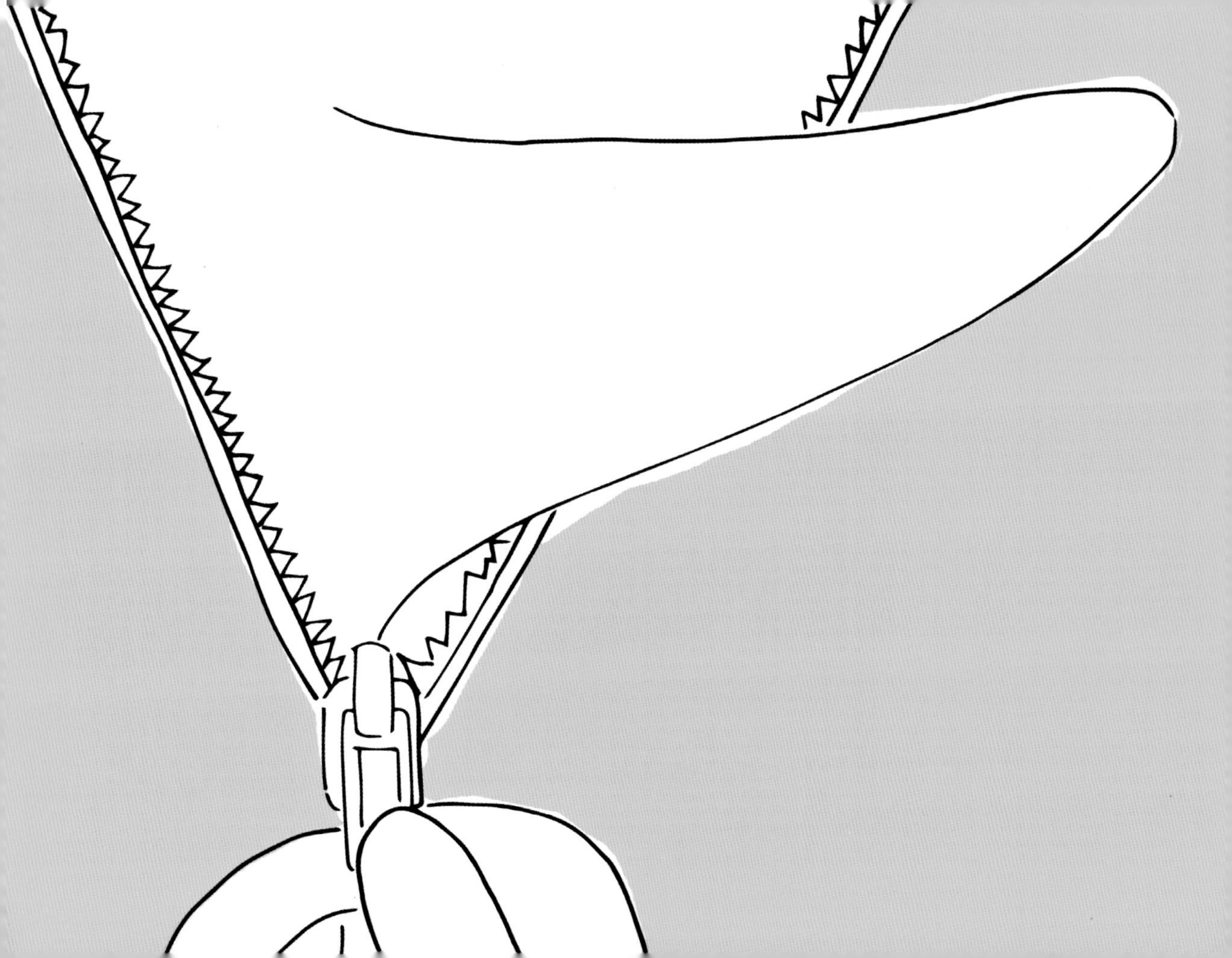

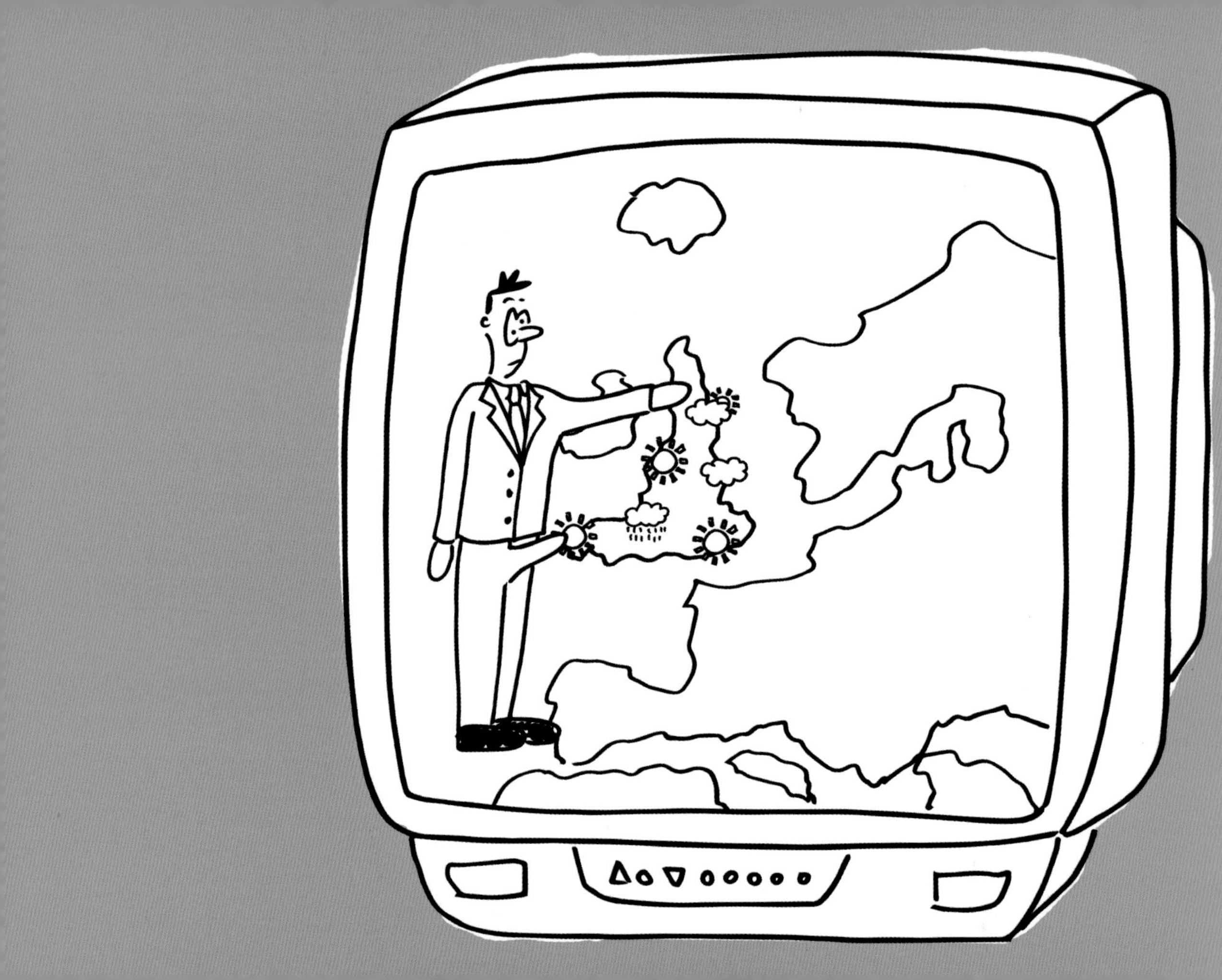

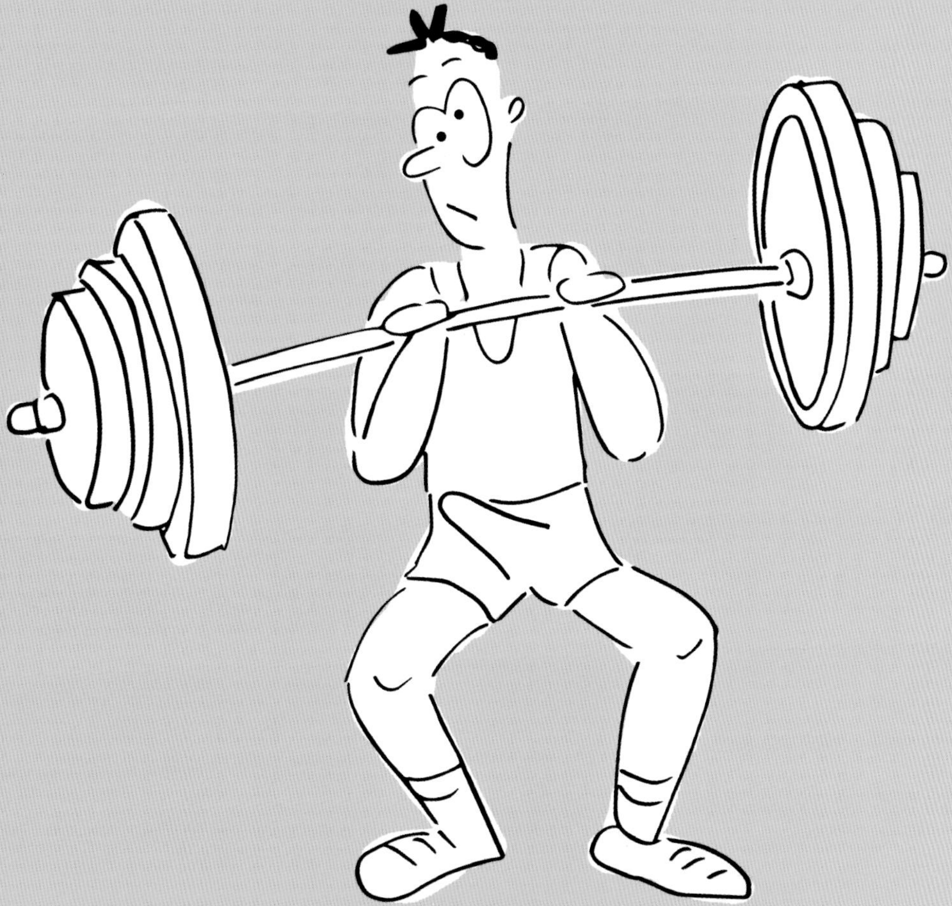

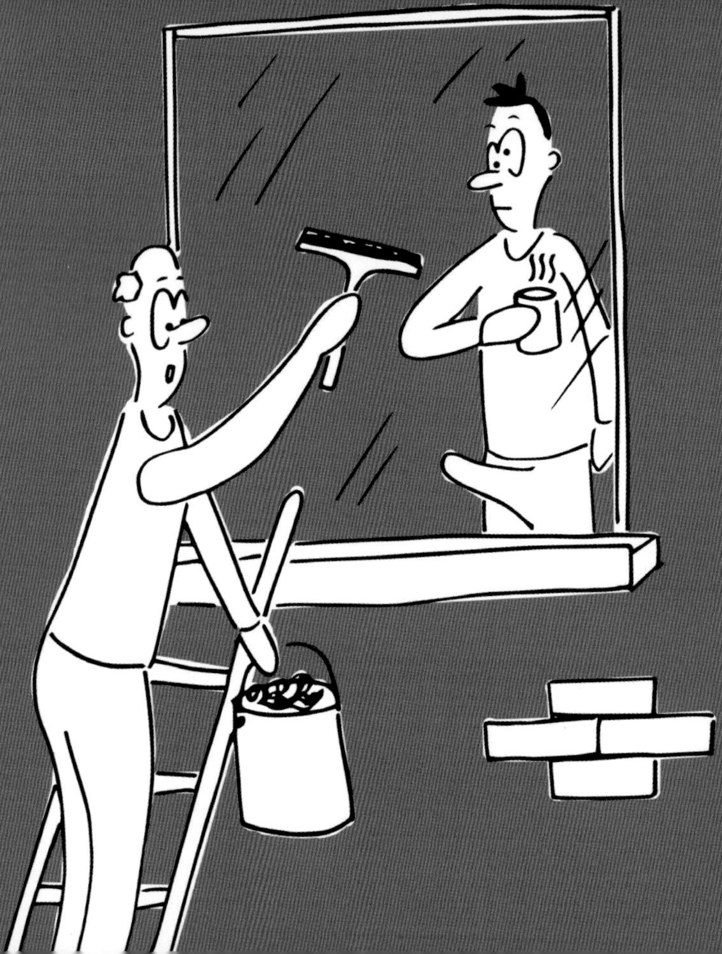

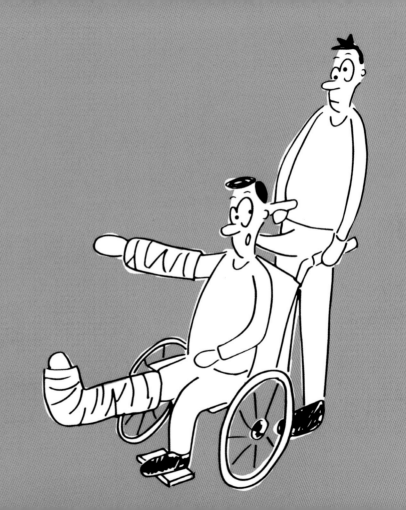

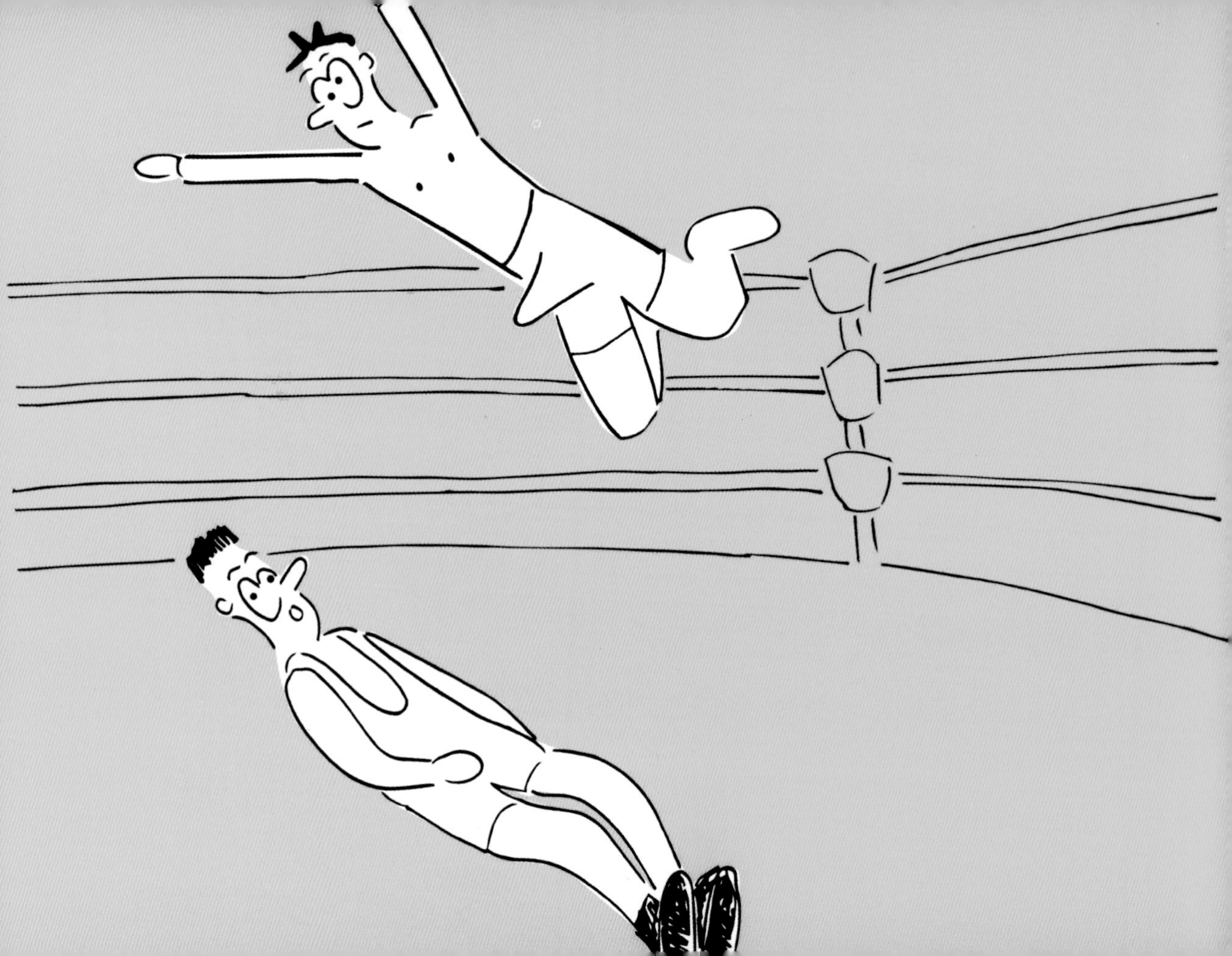

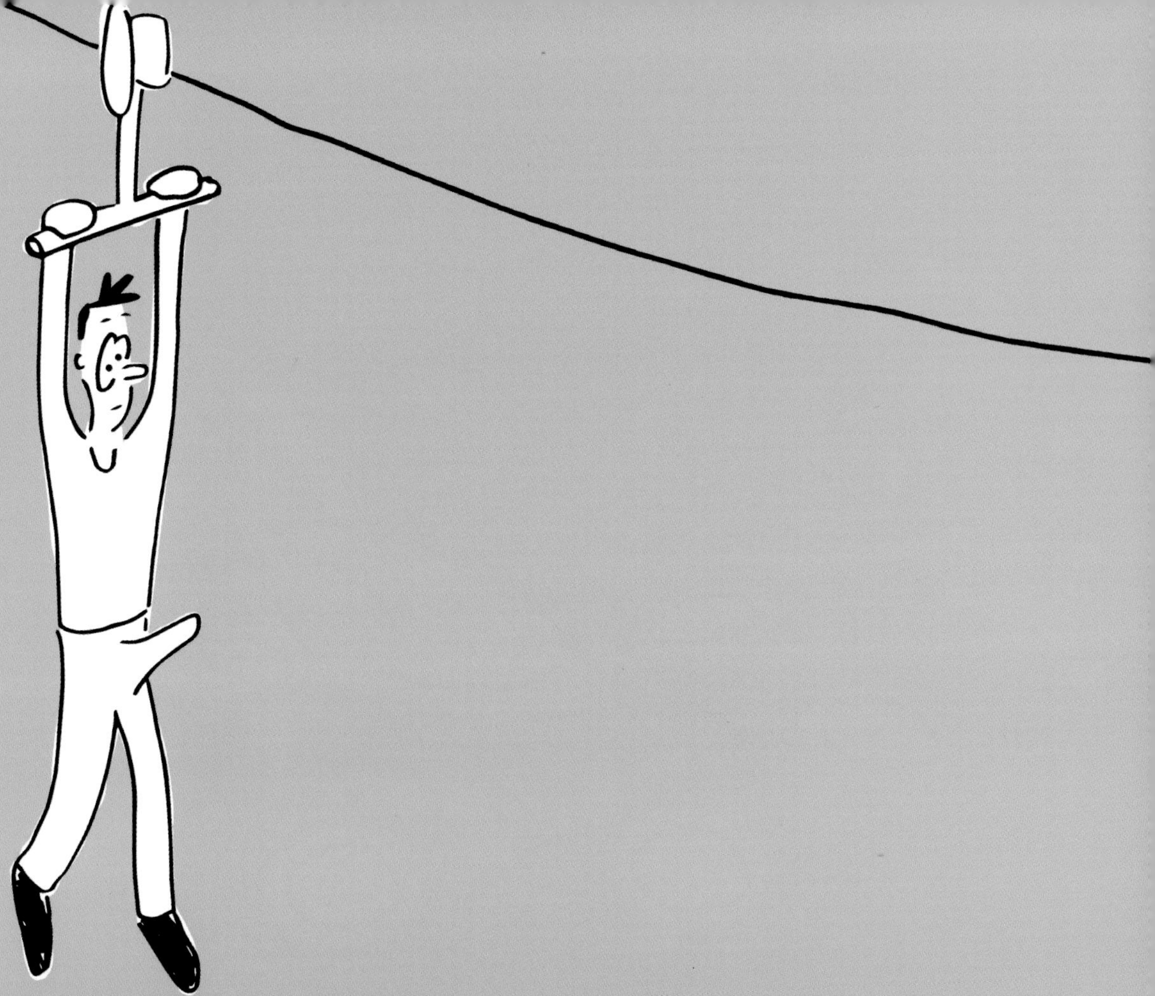

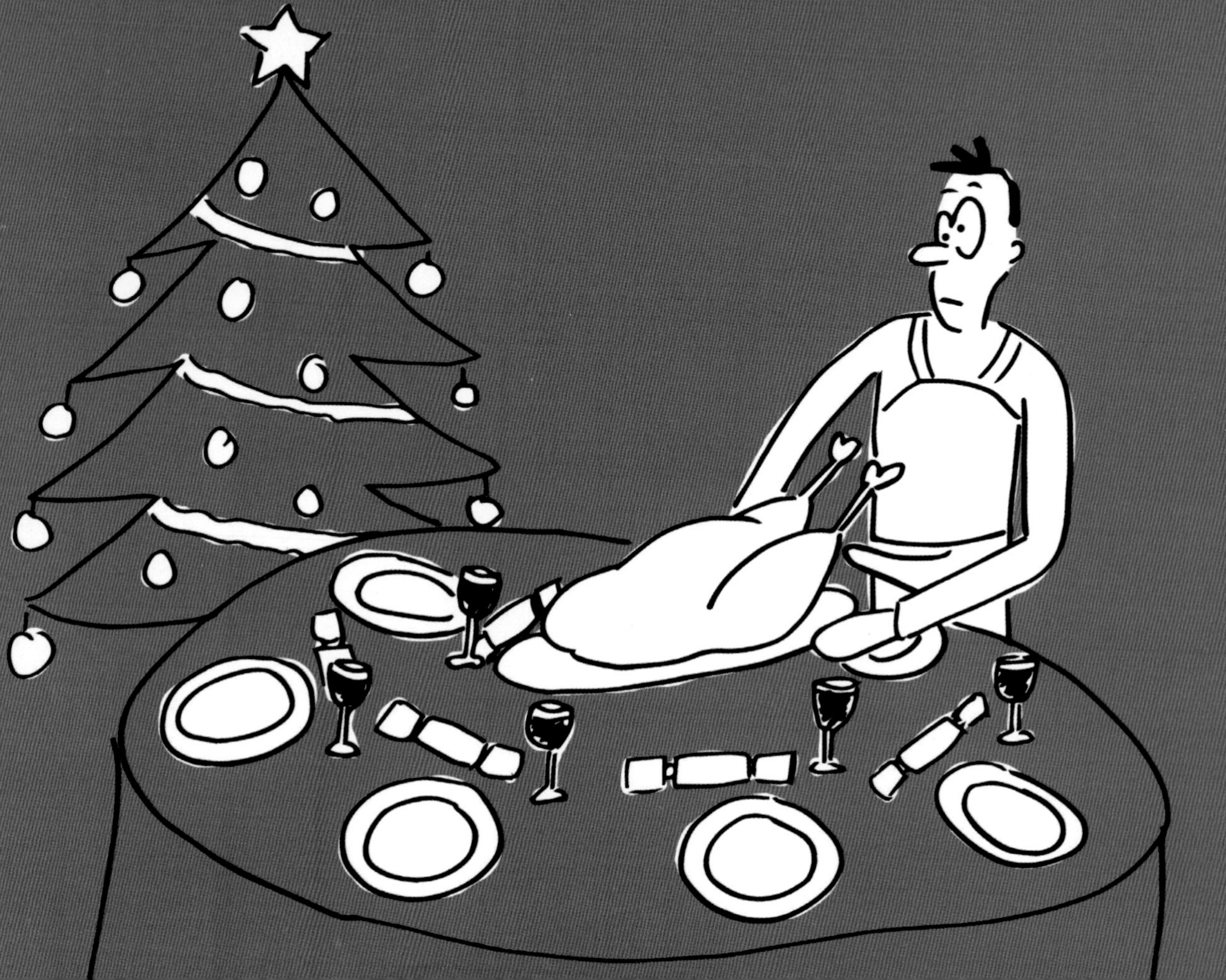

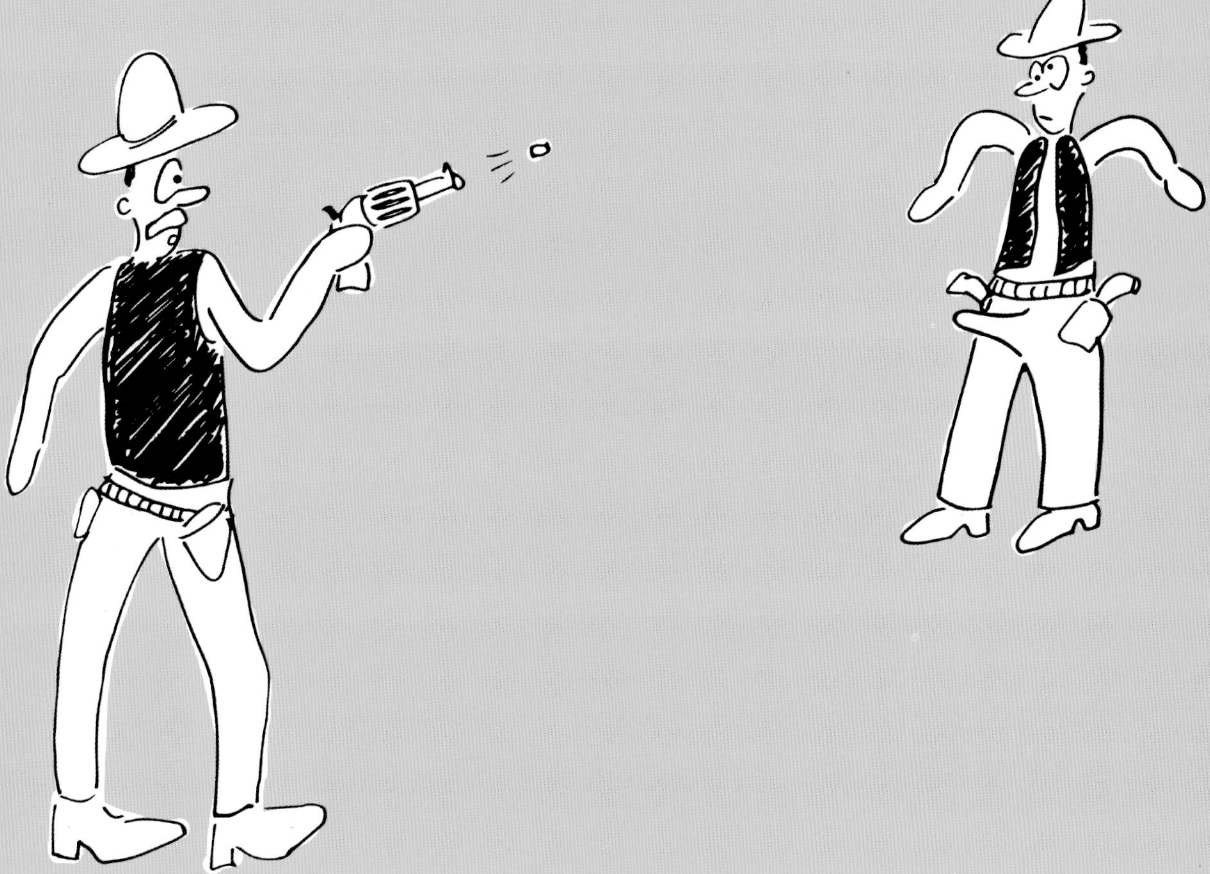

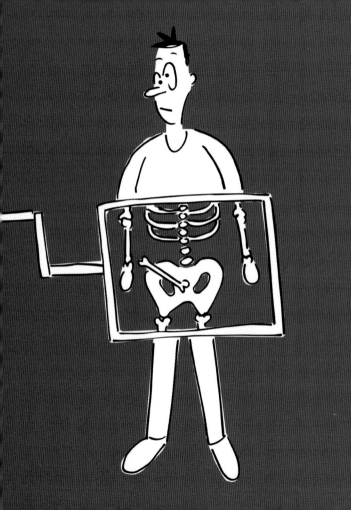

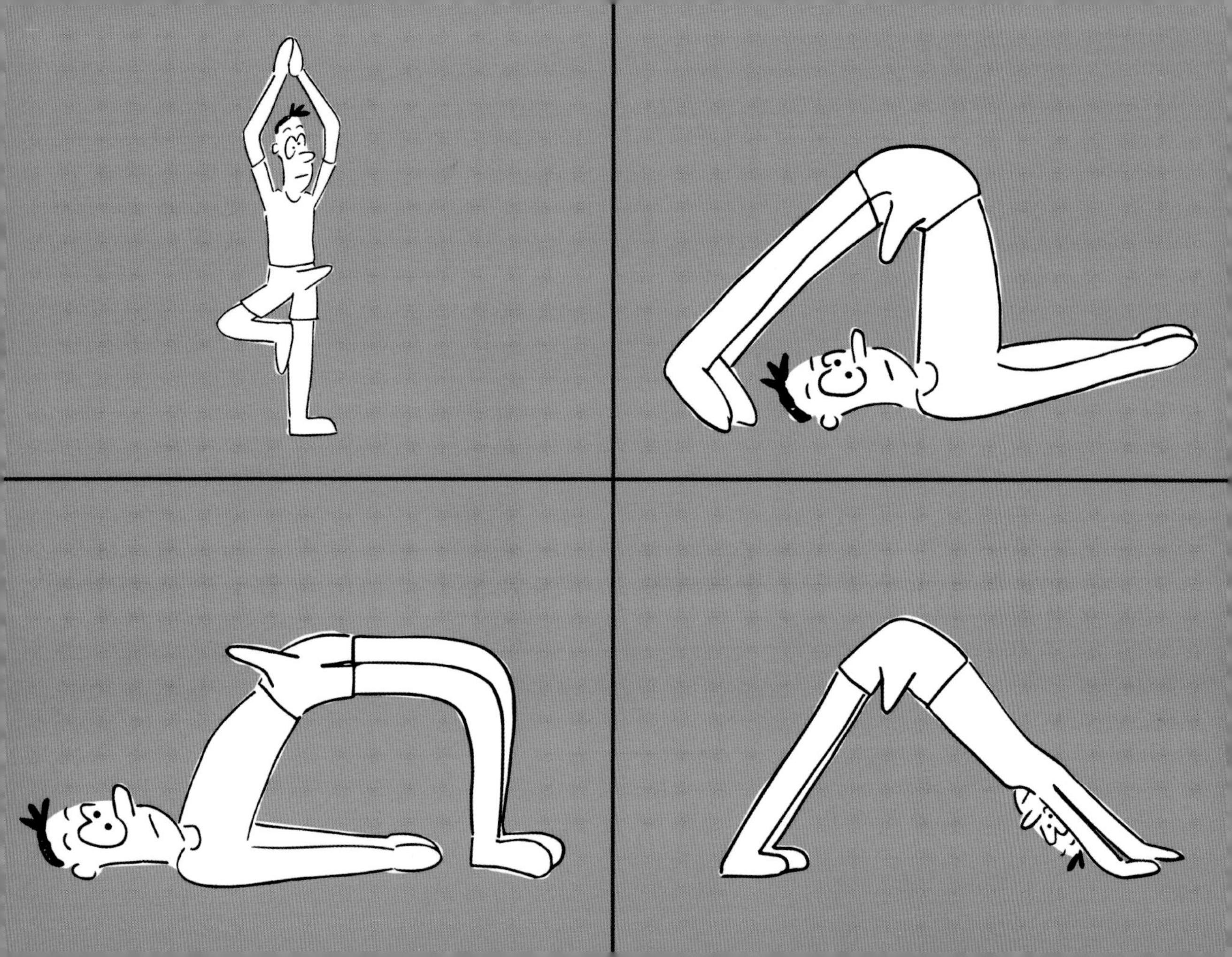

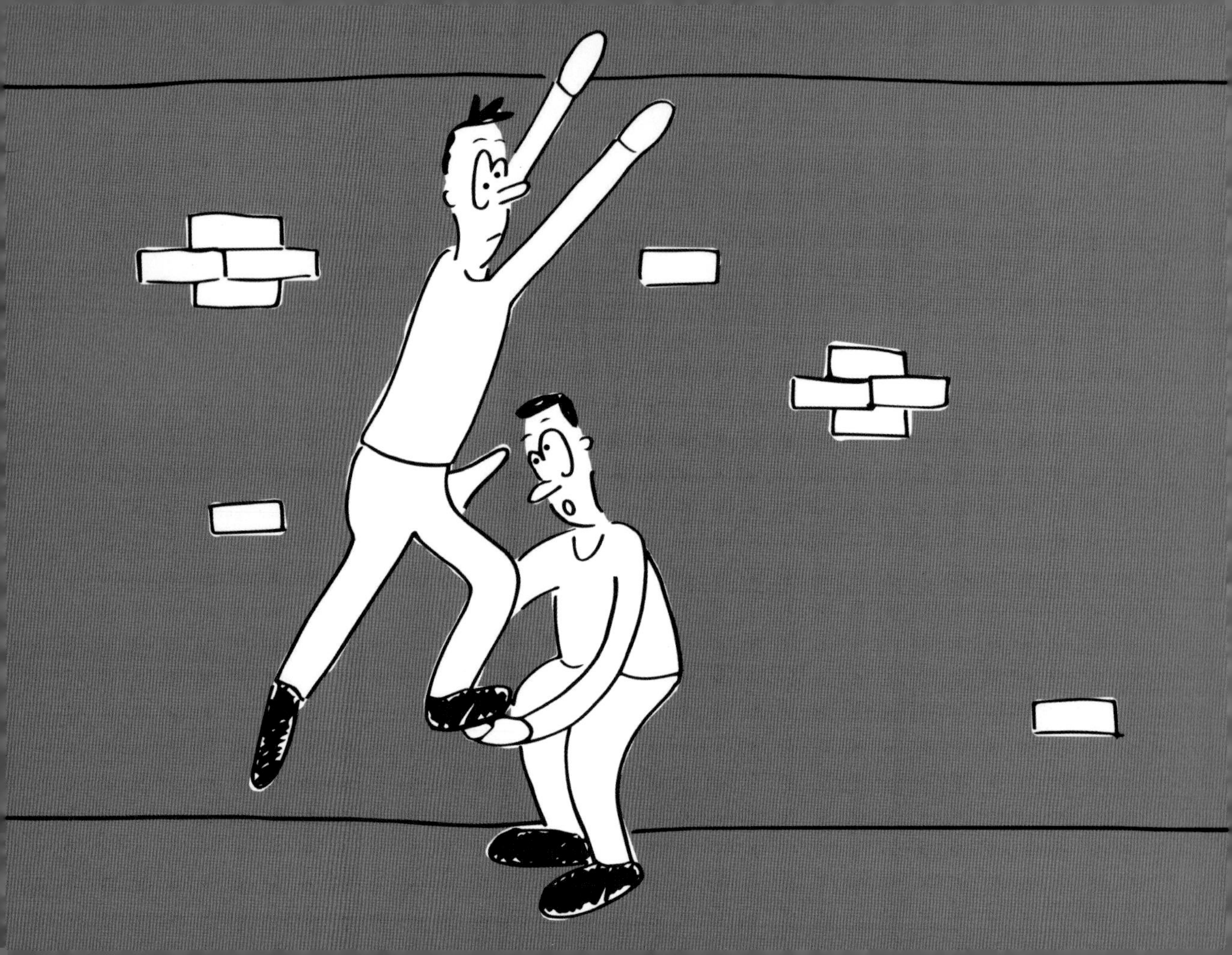

by Jolyon White

Photograph by Patrick Larder

Jolyon White (born July 22, 1983) studied graphic design and works for a creative advertising agency as an art director/copywriter. As well as drawing boners, Jolyon has worked as a chef, been part of a world-class rowing programme and even tried his hand at standup comedy. His girlfriend is very proud of him but also slightly concerned about his mild obsession with erections. He found it very difficult to tell his parents about this book and dreads the day he has to explain it to his future children.